PERMANENT RECORD

HOW ONE MAN EXPOSED THE TRUTH ABOUT
GOVERNMENT SPYING AND DIGITAL SECURITY

All Power to the Councils!
A Documentary History of the
German Revolution of 1918–1919

Edited and translated by Gabriel Kuhn

ISBN: 978-1-60486-111-2
$26.95   352 pages

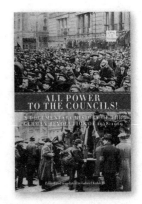

The German Revolution erupted out of the ashes of
World War I, triggered by mutinying sailors refusing to
be sacrificed in the final carnage of the war. While the
Social Democrats grabbed power, radicals across the country rallied to establish
a communist society under the slogan "All Power to the Councils!" The Spartacus
League launched an uprising in Berlin, council republics were proclaimed in
Bremen and Bavaria, and workers' revolts shook numerous German towns. Yet
in an act that would tragically shape the course of history, the Social Democratic
government crushed the rebellions with the help of right-wing militias, paving the
way for the ill-fated Weimar Republic—and ultimately the ascension of the Nazis.

This definitive documentary history collects manifestos, speeches, articles,
and letters from the German Revolution—Rosa Luxemburg, the Revolutionary
Stewards, and Gustav Landauer amongst others—introduced and annotated by the
editor. Many documents, such as the anarchist Erich Mühsam's comprehensive
account of the Bavarian Council Republic, are presented here in English for the first
time. The volume also includes materials from the Red Ruhr Army that repelled the
reactionary Kapp Putsch in 1920 and the communist bandits that roamed Eastern
Germany until 1921. *All Power to the Councils!* provides a dynamic and vivid picture
of a time of great hope and devastating betrayal.

*"Gabriel Kuhn's excellent volume illuminates a profound global revolutionary moment,
in which brilliant ideas and debates lit the sky."*
—Marcus Rediker, author of *Villains of All Nations* and *The Slave Ship*

*"This remarkable collection, skillfully edited by Gabriel Kuhn, brings to life that most
pivotal of revolutions, crackling with the acrid odor of street fighting, insurgent hopes,
and ultimately defeat… In an era brimming with anticapitalist aspirations, these pages
ring with that still unmet revolutionary promise of a better world: I was, I am, I shall
be."*
—Sasha Lilley, author of *Capital and Its Discontents* and coauthor of *Catastrophism*

*"Drawing on newly uncovered material through pioneering archival historical research,
Gabriel Kuhn's powerful book on the German workers' councils movement is essential
reading to understanding the way forward for democratic worker control today."*
—Immanuel Ness, Graduate Center for Worker Education, Brooklyn College

The Unknown Revolution: 1917-1921

Voline with an Introduction by Iain McKay and Foreword by Rudolf Rocker

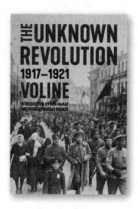

ISBN: 978-1-62963-577-4
$32.95   832 pages

This is the untold story of the Russian Revolution: its antecedents, its far-reaching changes, its betrayal by Bolshevik terror, and the massive resistance of non-Bolshevik revolutionaries. This in-depth, eyewitness history written by Voline, an outspoken activist in the Russian Revolution, is accompanied by a biography of the author by Rudolf Rocker and a contemporary introduction by anarchist historian Iain McKay.

Significant attention is given to what the author describes as "struggles for the real Social Revolution"; that is, the uprising of the sailors and workers of Kronstadt in 1921, and the peasant movement that Nestor Makhno led in Ukraine. These movements, which sought to defend the social revolution from destruction by the politicians, provide important material for a clearer understanding of both the original objectives of the Russian Revolution and the problems with which all revolutions with far-reaching social objectives have to contend.

Drawing on the revolutionary press of the time, Voline reveals the deep cleavage between the objectives of the libertarians and those of the Bolsheviks, differences which the latter "resolved" by ruthlessly eliminating all who stood in their way in the struggle for power.

This edition is a translation of the full text of *La Révolution inconnue*, originally published in French in 1947. It reinstates material omitted from earlier English-language editions and reproduces the complete text of the original volumes.

"A fascinating and valuable book—a combination of history, eyewitness account, and partisan advocacy—about the Russian revolution of 1917-21."
—Stephen F. Cohen, author of *Bukharin and the Bolshevik Revolution*

"In rich detail Voline documents the efforts of workers, peasants, and intellectuals to inaugurate a free society based on local initiative and autonomy. . . . It should be read by every person interested in the anarchist movement and the Russian Revolution."
—Paul Avrich, author of *The Russian Anarchists*

PERMANENT RECORD

Young Readers Edition

HOW One Man Exposed THE TruTH aBOuT
Government spyinG anD DIGITaL securiTy

EDWARD SNOWDEN

HENRY HOLT AND COMPANY

NEW YORK

Henry Holt and Company, *Publishers since 1866*
Henry Holt® is a registered trademark of Macmillan Publishing Group, LLC
120 Broadway, New York, NY 10271 • mackids.com

Library of Congress Cataloging-in-Publication Data

Names: Snowden, Edward J., 1983- author.
Title: Permanent record : how one man exposed the truth about government
    spying and digital security / Edward Snowden.
Description: Young readers edition, First edition. | New York : Henry Holt and
    Company, 2021. | Includes bibliographical references. | Audience: Ages 10-14 |
    Summary: "In 2013, Edward Snowden shocked the world when he broke with the
    American intelligence establishment and revealed that the United States government
    was secretly pursuing the means to collect every single phone call, text message, and
    email. The result would be an unprecedented system of mass surveillance with the
    ability to pry into the private lives of every person on earth. Six years later, the man
    who risked everything to expose the US government's system of mass surveillance
    reveals to a new generation how he helped build that system, what motivated him
    to try to bring it down, and how kids can protect their privacy in this digital age of
    indiscriminate data collection"— Provided by publisher.
Identifiers: LCCN 2020022084 | ISBN 9781250767912 (hardcover)
Subjects: LCSH: Snowden, Edward J., 1983—Juvenile literature. | Whistle blowing—
    United States—Juvenile literature. | Leaks (Disclosure of information)—United
    States—Juvenile literature. | Electronic surveillance—United States—Juvenile literature.
    | United States. National Security Agency—Officials and employees—Juvenile
    literature. | Government information—United States—Juvenile literature.
Classification: LCC JF1525.W45 S65 2021 | DDC 327.12730092—dc23
LC record available at https://lccn.loc.gov/2020022084

Our books may be purchased in bulk for promotional, educational, or business use.
Please contact your local bookseller or the Macmillan Corporate and Premium
Sales Department at (800) 221-7945 ext. 5442 or by email at
MacmillanSpecialMarkets@macmillan.com.

First edition, 2021 / Designed by Liz Dresner
Printed in the United States of America by LSC Communications,
Harrisonburg, Virginia

10 9 8 7 6 5 4 3 2

To L

CONTENTS

FOREWORD

THE FOURTH AMENDMENT TO THE US CONSTITUTION protects people and their property from government scrutiny. It states: *The right of the people to be secure in their persons, houses, papers, and effects, against unreasonable searches and seizures, shall not be violated, and no Warrants shall issue, but upon probable cause, supported by Oath or affirmation, and particularly describing the place to be searched, and the persons or things to be seized.*

Translation: If officers of the law want to go rooting through your life, they first have to go before a judge and explain why. They have to establish that they have reason to believe that you might have committed a specific crime, or that they believe specific evidence of a specific crime might be found on or in a specific part of your property. They have to swear that this reason has been given honestly and in good faith.

Only if the judge approves a warrant will they be allowed to go searching—and even then, only for a limited time.

The Constitution was written in the eighteenth century, back before computers were invented. It stands to reason that computer files, whatever their contents, are our version of the Constitution's "papers." Data, meanwhile, is our version of "effects," a catchall term for all the stuff that we own, produce, sell, and buy online.

In the centuries since the original Constitution Day, our clouds, computers, and phones have become our homes, just as personal and intimate as our actual houses nowadays. If you don't agree, then answer me this: Would you rather let your friends hang out in your bedroom alone for an hour, or let them spend even just ten minutes alone with your unlocked phone?

PREFACE

MY name is Edward Joseph Snowden. I used to work for the United States government, but now I work for you, the public. It took me nearly three decades to recognize that there was a distinction. I spend my time trying to protect the public from the person I used to be—a spy for the Central Intelligence Agency (CIA) and National Security Agency (NSA).

The reason you're reading this book is that I did a dangerous thing for a man in my position: I decided to tell the truth about my country's secret regime of mass surveillance. A system of near-universal surveillance had been set up not just without the American public's consent, but in a way that deliberately hid every aspect of its programs from our knowledge. In other words, the government sworn to protect its citizens was also spying on them.

When the program was first created—when I helped build it—I didn't realize that engineering a system that would keep a permanent record of everyone's life would turn out to be a tragic mistake. But over time, I came to understand that American citizens were being surveilled in a way that went against not just the Constitution of the United States, but the basic values of any free society. The public had never been granted a chance to voice our opinion about this surveillance.

I love my country, and I believe in public service—my whole family, my whole family line for centuries, is filled with men and women who have spent their lives serving this country and its citizens. I had sworn an oath of service to the public, in support and defense of the Constitution, whose guarantee of civil liberties had been blatantly violated. I realized that coming forward and disclosing the extent of my country's abuses was critical. I therefore decided to become what's known as a whistleblower.

In 2013, I collected internal Intelligence Community documents that gave evidence of the US government's lawbreaking and turned them over to journalists, who vetted and published them. In doing so, I knew I could—and would—be charged with crimes by the US government under the Espionage Act. The penalty for disclosing top secret documents, whether to foreign spies or domestic journalists, is up to ten years imprisonment per document. As a result, I have lived in exile in Moscow, Russia, a country I did not choose, for more than seven years.

This book is about what led up to that decision, the moral and ethical principles that informed it, and the impact that mass surveillance and data collection continues to have on all of us.

It's also about my life.

PART ONE

one

Looking Through the Window

THE FIRST THING I EVER HACKED WAS BEDTIME.
When I was young, it always felt unfair that my parents forced me to go to sleep before they or my sister did. I wasn't even tired. Life's first little injustice.

Many nights of the first several years of my life ended in civil disobedience: crying, begging, bargaining. Until the night I turned six and discovered direct action.

I had just had one of the best days of my life, complete with friends, a party, and gifts, and I wasn't about to let it end. So I went about covertly resetting all the clocks in the house by several hours, trying to trick my parents into thinking it was earlier in the evening.

When the authorities—my parents—failed to notice, I was mad with power, galloping laps around the living room. I, the master of time, would never again be sent to bed. I was free.

I fell asleep on the floor, having finally seen the sunset on June 21, the summer solstice, the longest day of the year. But when I awoke, the clocks in the house once again matched my father's watch.

If you're like most people these days, you set your watch, if you wear one, to the time on your smartphone. But if you look at your phone, and I mean really look at it, burrowing deep through its menus into its settings, you'll eventually see that the phone's time is "automatically set." Every so often, your phone quietly—silently—asks your service provider's network, "Hey, do you have the time?" That network, in turn, asks a bigger network, which asks an even bigger network, and so on through a great succession of towers and wires until the request reaches one of the true masters of time, a network time server run by the atomic clocks kept at places like the National Institute of Standards and Technology in the United States, the Federal Office of Meteorology and Climatology in Switzerland, and the National Institute of Information and Communications Technology in Japan. That long invisible journey, accomplished in a fraction of a second, is why you don't see a blinking *12:00* on your phone's screen every time you power it up again after its battery runs out.

I was born in 1983, at the end of the era in which people set the time for themselves. That was the year that the US Department of Defense created a computer network for the public called the internet. This virtual space gave rise to the Domain Name System that we still use today—the .govs, .mils, .edus, and, of course, .coms. And yet it would be another six years before the World Wide Web was invented, and about nine years before my family got a computer with a modem that could connect to it.

Of course, the internet is not a single entity, although we tend to refer to it as if it were. I'm going to use the term in its broadest sense, to mean the universal network of networks connecting the majority of the world's computers to one another via a set of shared protocols.

Don't worry if you think you don't know a protocol from a hole in the wall. You've used them without knowing it. Think of protocols as languages for machines, the common rules they follow to be understood by one another. Every time you check your email, you use a language like IMAP (Internet Message Access Protocol) or SMTP (Simple Mail Transfer Protocol). And the time-setting procedure on your phone that I mentioned uses NTP (Network Time Protocol).

The takeaway is this: These protocols have given us the means to digitize just about everything. The internet has become almost as integral to our lives as the air through which so many of its communications travel. And to digitize something is to record it in a format that will last forever.

Here's what strikes me when I think back to my childhood, particularly those first nine internet-less years: I can't account for everything that happened back then, because I have only my memory to rely on. My generation is the last in American, and perhaps even in world, history whose childhoods aren't up on the cloud. They're mostly trapped in analog formats like handwritten diaries and Polaroid cameras. My schoolwork was done on paper with pencils and erasers, not on networked tablets that logged my keystrokes. My growth spurts weren't tracked by smart-home technologies, but notched with a knife into the wood of the door frame of the house in which I grew up.

•   •   •   •   •   •   •

We lived in a grand old redbrick house on a little patch of lawn shaded by dogwoods and magnolias. Their flowers often served as cover for the plastic army men I used to crawl around with. The house had an atypical layout: Its main entrance was on the second floor, accessed by a massive brick staircase. This floor was the primary living space, with the kitchen, dining room, and bedrooms.

Above this main floor was a dusty, cobwebbed, and forbidding attic, haunted by what my mother promised me were squirrels, but what my father insisted were vampire werewolves that would devour any child foolish enough to venture up there. Below the main floor was a more or less finished basement.

My bedroom, which was part of an addition to the house, had a view of the den through a window in what had originally been the exterior wall of the house. This window, which once looked outside, now looked inside.

Though the window had a curtain, it didn't provide much privacy. From as far back as I can remember, my favorite activity was to tug the curtain aside and peek through it into the den. Which is to say, from as far back as I can remember, my favorite activity was spying.

I spied on my older sister, Jessica, who was allowed to stay up later than I was and watch the cartoons that I was still too young for. I spied on my mother, who'd sit on the couch to fold the laundry while watching the nightly news. But the person I spied on the most was my father, who'd commandeer the den into the wee hours.

My father was in the Coast Guard. He sometimes wore a uniform and sometimes didn't. He left home early and came home late, often with new gadgets, some of which he'd show me and some of which he'd hide. Which would you be more interested in?

The gadget that most caught my eye arrived one night just after I was supposed to be asleep. I was about to drift off when I heard my father's footsteps coming down the hall. I stood up on my bed, tugged aside the curtain, and watched. He was holding a mysterious box the size of a shoebox, and he removed from it a beige object that looked like a cinder block. Long black cables snaked out of it like the tentacles of some deep-sea monster from one of my nightmares.

Working slowly and methodically—which was partially his disciplined, engineer's way of doing everything and partially an attempt to stay quiet—my father untangled the cables and stretched one across the shag carpet from the back of the box to the back of the TV. Then he plugged the other cable into a wall outlet behind the couch.

Suddenly, the TV lit up, and with it my father's face lit up, too. Normally, he spent his evenings sitting on the couch, cracking sodas and watching the people on TV run around a field, but this was different. *My father was controlling what was happening on TV.*

I had come face-to-face with a Commodore 64—one of the first home computer systems on the market.

At the time, I had no idea what a computer was, as

they were not yet widespread like they are today. I knew only one thing: Whatever he was doing, I wanted to do it, too.

After that, whenever my father came into the den to break out the beige brick, I'd stand up on my bed, tug away the curtain, and spy on his adventures. One night I was truly confused by what he was doing—was it for fun or was it part of his job?—when I peeked through the window and saw him *flying*.

My father was piloting his own helicopter right there, right in front of me, in our den, on the TV screen. He took off from a little base, complete with a tiny waving American flag, into a black night sky full of twinkling stars, and then immediately crashed to the ground. He gave a little cry that masked my own, but just when I thought the fun was over, he was right back at the little base again with the tiny flag, taking off one more time.

The game was called *Choplifter!* and it was thrilling. Again and again the helicopter landed and lifted off as my father tried to rescue a flashing crowd of people and ferry them to safety. That was my earliest sense of my father: He was a hero.

The first time he landed that helicopter intact with a full load of miniature people, he cheered just a little too loud. His head snapped to the window to check whether he'd disturbed me, and he caught me dead in the eyes.

I leaped into bed, pulled up the blanket, and lay perfectly still as my father's heavy steps approached my room.

He tapped on the window. "It's past your bedtime, buddy. Are you still up?"

I held my breath. Suddenly he opened the window, reached in, picked me up—blanket and all—and pulled me through into the den. It all happened so quickly, my feet never even touched the carpet.

Before I knew it, I was sitting on my father's lap as his copilot. I was too excited to realize that the joystick he'd given me wasn't plugged in. All that mattered was that I was flying alongside my father.

TWO

The Invisible Wall

Elizabeth City, North Carolina, is a quaint, midsize town built up around the banks of the Pasquotank River. My family has always been connected to the sea, my mother's side in particular. Her heritage is straight Pilgrim—her first ancestor on these shores was John Alden, the *Mayflower*'s cooper, or barrel maker. He became the husband of a fellow passenger named Priscilla Mullins, who was the only single woman of marriageable age onboard.

John and Priscilla's daughter, Elizabeth, was the first Pilgrim girl born in New England. My mother, whose name is also Elizabeth (though she often goes by Wendy), is her direct descendant.

My maternal grandfather, whom I call Pop, is better known as Rear Admiral Edward J. Barrett. At the time of my birth he was deputy chief, aeronautical engineering division, Coast Guard Headquarters, Washington, DC. He'd go on to hold various engineering and operational commands. I wasn't aware of how high up the ranks Pop was rising, but I knew that the welcome-to-command ceremonies became more elaborate as time went on, with longer speeches and larger cakes. I remember the souvenir I was given by the artillery guard at one of them: the shell casing of a 40 mm round, still warm and smelling like powdered hell, which had just been fired in a salute in Pop's honor.

Then there's my father, Lon, who at the time of my birth was a chief petty officer at the Coast Guard's Aviation Technical Training Center in Elizabeth City, working as a curriculum designer and electronics instructor. He was often away, leaving my mother at home to raise my sister and me. To give us a sense of responsibility, she gave us chores; to teach us how to read, she labeled all our dresser drawers with their contents—socks, underwear. She would load us into our Red Flyer wagon and tow us to the local library. As a kid, my favorite section was the one that I pronounced "big masheens." Whenever my mother asked me if I was interested in any specific "big masheen," I was unstoppable: "Dump trucks and steam-rollers and forklifts and cranes and—"

"Is that all, buddy?"

"Oh," I'd say, "and also cement mixers and bulldozers and—"

My mother loved giving me math challenges. While shopping at Kmart or Winn-Dixie, she'd have me pick out books and model cars and trucks and buy them for me if I was able to add up their prices in my head. Over the course of my childhood, she kept escalating the difficulty, first having me round to the nearest dollar, then having me figure out the precise dollar-and-cents amount, and then having me calculate 3 percent of that amount and add it on to the total. I was confused by that last challenge—not by the arithmetic so much as by the reasoning. "Why?"

"It's called tax," my mother explained. "Everything we buy, we have to pay three percent to the government."

"What do they do with it?"

"You like roads, buddy? You like bridges?" she said. "The government uses that money to fix them. They use that money to fill the library with books."

Some time later, I was afraid that my budding math skills had failed me, when my mental totals didn't match those on the cash register's display. But once again, my mother explained, "They raised the sales tax. Now you have to add four percent."

"So now the library will get even more books?" I asked.

"Let's hope," my mother said.

When I wasn't using my math skills in exchange for prizes, I'd often go to my grandmother's house, which was a few streets over from us, and lie on the carpet beside the long, low bookshelves. My usual company was an edition of *Aesop's Fables* and, perhaps my favorite, *Bulfinch's Mythology*. I was in awe of the hero of Greek mythology named Odysseus and liked Zeus, Apollo, Hermes, and Athena well enough, but the deity I admired most had to be Hephaestus: the ugly god of fire, volcanoes, blacksmiths, and carpenters, the god of tinkerers. I was proud of being able to spell his Greek name, and of knowing that his Roman name, Vulcan, was used for the home planet of Spock from *Star Trek*.

Once, I picked up an illustrated version of the legends of King Arthur and his knights and found myself reading about the fortress of a tyrannical giant named Rhitta Gawr, who refused to accept that the age of his reign had passed and that in the future the world would be ruled by human kings.

The giant lived on a mountain called Snaw Dun, which, a note explained, was Old English for "snow mound." Today, Snaw Dun is called Mount Snowdon. I remember the feeling of encountering my last name in this context—it was thrilling—and the archaic spelling gave me my first sense that the world was older than I was, even older than my parents were.

Years later, I was obsessed with a new and different type of storytelling. On Christmas 1989, a Nintendo appeared in the house. I took to that two-tone-gray video game console so completely that my alarmed mother imposed a rule: I could only rent a new game when I finished reading a book. Games were expensive, and, having already mastered the ones that had come with the console—a single cartridge combining *Super Mario Bros.* and *Duck Hunt*—I was eager for other challenges. I started coming home from the library with shorter books and books with lots of pictures, including visual encyclopedias of inventions and comic books.

It was the NES—the janky but genius eight-bit Nintendo Entertainment System—that was my real education. From *The Legend of Zelda* I learned that the world exists to be explored; from *Mega Man* I learned that my enemies have much to teach; and from *Duck Hunt*—well, *Duck Hunt* taught me that even if someone laughs at your failures, it doesn't mean you get to shoot them in the face.

Ultimately, though, it was *Super Mario Bros.* that taught me what remains perhaps the most important lesson of my life. *Super Mario Bros.*, the 1.0 edition, is perhaps the all-time masterpiece of side-scrolling games.

When the game begins, Mario is standing all the way to the left of the legendary opening screen, and he can only go in one direction: He can only move to the right as new scenery and enemies scroll in from that side. He progresses through eight worlds of four levels each, all of them governed by time constraints, until he reaches the evil Bowser and frees the captive Princess Toadstool.

Throughout all thirty-two levels, Mario exists in front of what in gaming speak is called "an invisible wall," which doesn't allow him to go backward. There is no turning back, only going forward—for Mario and Luigi, for me, and for you. Life only scrolls in one direction, which is the direction of time, and no matter how far we might manage to go, that invisible wall will always be just behind us, cutting us off from the past, compelling us on into the unknown future.

One day, my much-used *Super Mario Bros.* cartridge wasn't loading, no matter how much I blew into it. That's what you had to do, or what we thought you had to do when a game would no longer load: You had to blow into the open mouth of the cartridge to clear it of the dust, debris, and pet hair that tended to accumulate there. But no matter how much I blew, the TV screen was full of blotches and waves, which were not reassuring in the least.

The Nintendo was probably just suffering from a faulty pin connection, but given that back then I didn't even know what a pin connection was, I was frustrated and desperate. Worst of all, my father had just left on a Coast Guard trip and wouldn't be back to help me fix it for two weeks. So I resolved to fix the thing myself. If I succeeded, I knew my father would be impressed. I went out to the garage to find his gray metal toolbox.

I decided that to figure out what was wrong with the thing, first I had to take it apart. Basically, I was just copying, or trying to copy, the same motions that my father went through whenever he sat at the kitchen table repairing other household machines that, to my eye, the Nintendo console most closely resembled. It took me about an hour to dismantle the console, with my uncoordinated and very small hands trying to twist a flat screwdriver into Phillips-head screws, but eventually I succeeded.

The console's exterior was a dull, monochrome gray, but the interior was a mass of colors. It seemed like there was an entire rainbow of wires and glints of silver and gold jutting out of the green-as-grass circuit board. I tightened a few things here, loosened a few things there—more or less at random—and blew on every part. After that, I wiped them all down with a paper towel. Then I had to blow on the circuit board again to remove the bits of paper towel that had gotten stuck to what I now know were the pins.

Once I'd finished my cleaning and repairs, it was

time for reassembly. Our dog, Treasure, might have swallowed one of the tiny screws, or maybe it had just gotten lost in the carpet or under the couch. And I must not have put all the components back in the same way I'd found them, because they barely fit into the console's shell. The shell's lid kept popping off, so I found myself squeezing the components down, the way you try to shut an overstuffed suitcase. Finally the lid snapped into place, but only on one side.

I pressed the power button—and nothing. I pressed the reset button—and nothing. Those were the only two buttons on the console. Before my repairs, the light next to the buttons had always glowed molten red, but now even that was dead. The console just sat there lopsided and useless, and I felt a surge of guilt and dread.

My father, when he came home from his Coast Guard trip, wasn't going to be proud of me: He was going to jump on my head like one of the Goombas in *Super Mario Bros.* But it wasn't his anger I feared so much as his disappointment. To his peers, my father was a master electronics systems engineer who specialized in avionics. To me, he was a household mad scientist who'd try to fix everything himself—electrical outlets, dishwashers, water heaters, and AC units. I'd work as his helper whenever he'd let me, and in the process I'd come to know both the physical pleasures of manual work and the intellectual pleasures of basic mechanics, along with the fundamental principles of electronics—the differences between voltage and current, between power and resistance. Every job we undertook together would end either in a successful act of repair or a curse as my father flung the unsalvageable piece of equipment across the room and into the cardboard box of things-that-can't-be-unbroken. I never judged him for these failures—I was always too impressed by the fact that he had dared to hazard an attempt.

When he returned home and found out what I'd done to the NES, he wasn't angry, much to my surprise. He wasn't exactly pleased, either, but he was patient. He explained that understanding why and how things had gone wrong was every bit as important as understanding what component had failed: figuring out the why and how would let you prevent the same malfunction from happening again in the future. He pointed to each of the console's parts in turn, explaining not just what it was, but what it did and how it interacted with all the other parts to contribute to the correct working of the mechanism. Only by analyzing individual parts could you determine whether a mechanism's design was the most efficient to achieve its task. If it was efficient, but malfunctioning, then you fixed it. But if it was inefficient, then you made modifications to improve the mechanism. This was the only proper protocol for repair jobs, according to my father, and nothing about it was optional—in fact, this was the fundamental responsibility you had to technology.

Like all my father's lessons, this one had broad applications beyond our immediate task. Ultimately, it was a lesson in the principle of self-reliance, which my father insisted that America had forgotten sometime between his own childhood and mine. Ours was now a country in which the cost of replacing a broken machine with a newer model was typically lower than the cost of having it fixed by an expert, which itself was typically lower than the cost of sourcing the parts and figuring out how to fix it yourself. Most people used technology daily and yet failed to understand the basic operation and maintenance of the equipment they depended on. It meant when their equipment worked, they worked, but when their equipment broke down, they broke down, too. Put another way, their possessions possessed them.

It turned out that I had probably just broken a solder joint, but to find out exactly which one, my father wanted to use special test equipment that he had access to at his laboratory at the Coast Guard base. I suppose he could have brought the test equipment home with him, but for some reason he brought me to work instead. I think he just wanted to show me his lab. He'd decided I was ready.

What I remember most are the screens. The lab itself was dim and empty, the standard-issue beige and white of government construction, but even before my father hit the lights I couldn't help but be transfixed by the pulsating glow of electric green. *Why does this place have so many TVs?* was my first thought, quickly followed up by, *And why are they all tuned to the same channel?* My father explained that these weren't TVs but computers.

He went on to show them to me, one by one, and tried to explain what they did: This one processed radar signals, and that one relayed radio transmissions, and yet another one simulated the electronic systems on aircraft. I won't pretend that I understood even half of it. These computers were more advanced than nearly everything in use at that time in the private sector. Sure, their processing units took a full five minutes to boot, their displays only showed one color, and they had no speakers for sound effects or music. But those limitations only marked them as serious.

My father plopped me down in a chair, and for the first time in my life, I found myself in front of a keyboard. But these computers were not gaming devices, and I didn't understand how to make them work. There was no controller, no joystick, no gun.

My father told me that every key on the keyboard had a purpose. To demonstrate, he reached over me, typed a command, and pressed the enter key. Something popped up on-screen that I now know is called a text editor. Then he grabbed a Post-it Note and a pen and scribbled out some letters and numbers. He told me to type them up exactly while he went off to repair the broken Nintendo.

The moment he was gone, I began pecking away at the keys. A left-handed kid raised to be a righty, I immediately found this to be the most natural method of writing I'd ever encountered.

10 input "what is your name?"; name$

20 print "hello, " + name$+ "!"

After a whole lot of trial, and a whole lot of error, I finally finished. I pressed enter, and, in a flash, the computer was asking me a question: *what is your name?*

I was fascinated. The note didn't say what I was supposed do next, so I decided to answer and pressed my new friend enter once more. Suddenly, out of nowhere, *hello, eddie!* wrote itself on-screen in a radioactive green that floated atop the blackness.

This was my introduction to computer programming: a lesson in the fact that these machines do what they do because somebody tells them to, in a very special, very careful way. And that somebody can be seven years old.

Almost immediately, I grasped the limitations of gaming systems. They were stifling in comparison to computer systems. They confined you to levels and worlds that you could advance through, even defeat, but never change.

The repaired Nintendo console went back to the den, where my father and I competed in two-player *Mario Kart, Double Dragon,* and *Street Fighter.* By that point, I was significantly better than him, but every so often, I'd let him beat me. I didn't want him to think that I wasn't grateful.

I'm not a natural programmer, and I've never considered myself any good at it. But I did, over the next decade or so, become good enough to be dangerous. I was fascinated by the thought that one individual programmer could code something universal, something bound by no laws or rules or regulations except cause and effect. There was an utterly logical relationship between my input and the output. If my input was flawed, the output was flawed; if my input was flawless, the computer's output was, too. I'd never before experienced anything so consistent and fair, so unequivocally unbiased. A computer would wait forever to receive my command but would process it the very moment I hit enter, no questions asked. Nowhere else had I ever felt so in control.

THREE

Beltway Boy

I was just shy of my ninth birthday when my family moved from North Carolina to Anne Arundel County in Maryland. To my surprise, I found the name Snowden everywhere. I only learned later that in 1686, England's King Charles II had granted my paternal ancestors nearly two thousand acres of land in the New World, much of which eventually became Anne Arundel County.

Today, the former Snowden fields are bisected by Snowden River Parkway, a busy four-lane commercial stretch. Nearby is Fort George G. Meade, the second-largest army base in the country and the home of the National Security Agency (NSA). Fort Meade, in fact, is built atop land that was once owned by my Snowden cousins.

I knew nothing of this history at the time: My parents joked that the state of Maryland changed the name on the signs every time somebody new moved in. They thought that was funny, but I just found it spooky. We'd only moved about 250 miles, yet it felt like a different planet. I had exchanged the leafy riverside for a concrete sidewalk, and a school where I'd been popular and academically successful for one where I was constantly mocked for my glasses, my disinterest in sports, and especially for my strong Southern drawl.

I was so sensitive about my accent that I stopped speaking in class and started practicing alone at home until I managed to sound "normal." Meanwhile, my grades plummeted, and some of my teachers decided to have me IQ-tested as a way of diagnosing what they thought was a learning disability. When my score came back, I don't remember getting any apologies, just a bunch of extra "enrichment assignments."

We lived in Crofton, Maryland, halfway between Annapolis and Washington, DC. Crofton itself is a planned community; on a map, it resembles the human brain, with the streets coiling and kinking and folding around one another. For my parents, this was an exciting time. Crofton was a step up for them, both economically and socially. Our backyard was basically a golf course, with tennis courts just around the corner, and beyond those an Olympic-size pool. It took my father just forty minutes to get to his new posting as a chief warrant officer in the Office of Aeronautical Engineering at Coast Guard Headquarters, which at the time was located at Buzzard Point in southern Washington, DC, adjacent to Fort Lesley J. McNair. And it took my mother just twenty or so minutes to get to her new job at the NSA, whose boxy futuristic headquarters forms the heart of Fort Meade.

As we lived so close to the headquarters of many government agencies, this type of employment was normal in our area. Neighbors to our left worked for the Defense Department; neighbors to the right worked in the Department of Energy and the Department of Commerce. For a while, nearly every girl at school on whom I had a crush had a father in the FBI.

For me, Fort Meade was just the place where my mother worked, along with about 125,000 other employees, approximately forty thousand of whom lived on-site, many with their families. The base was home to over 115 government agencies in addition to forces from all five branches of the military. The base has its own post offices, schools, police, and fire departments. Area children, military brats and civilians alike, would flock there daily to take golf, tennis, and swimming lessons. Though we lived off base, my mother still used its commissary as our grocery store to stock up on items in bulk. She also took advantage of the base's PX, or post exchange, as a one-stop shop for tax-free clothing for my sister and me.

Both my parents had top secret clearances, but my mother also had a higher-level security check that members of the military aren't subject to. My mother was the furthest thing from a spy. She was a clerk at an independent insurance association that serviced employees of the NSA—she provided spies with retirement plans. But still, she had to be vetted as if she were about to parachute into a jungle to stage a coup.

My father's career remains fairly murky to me to this day. In the world I grew up in, nobody really talked about their jobs—not just to children, but to each other. Tech people rarely, if ever, have a sense of the broader purposes of the projects to which they're assigned. And the work that consumes them tends to require such specialized knowledge that to bring it up at a barbecue would get them disinvited from the next one, because nobody cared.

In retrospect, maybe that secrecy led to the problems we currently face.

Four

American Online

IT WAS SOON AFTER WE MOVED TO CROFTON that my father brought home our first desktop computer and set it up—much to my mother's chagrin—smack in the middle of the dining room table. From the moment it appeared, the computer and I were inseparable. It had what at the time felt like an impossibly fast 25-megahertz Intel 486 CPU and a color monitor that could display up to 256 different colors. (Your current device can probably display in the millions.) It was amazing.

This computer became my constant companion. My parents would call my name to tell me to get ready for school, but I wouldn't hear them. They'd call my

name to tell me to wash up for dinner, but I'd pretend not to hear them. And whenever I was reminded
that the computer was a shared computer and not my
personal machine, I'd relinquish my seat with such
reluctance that as my father or mother or sister took
their turn, they'd have to order me out of the room
entirely lest I hover moodily over their shoulders and
offer advice.

I'd try to rush them through their tasks, so I could
get back to mine, which were so much more important—
like playing *Loom*. *Loom* was about a society of Weavers
whose elders create a secret loom that controls the
world. When a young boy discovers the loom's power,
he's forced into exile, and everything spirals into chaos
until the world decides that a secret fate machine might
not be such a great idea after all.

Unbelievable, sure. But then again, it's just a game.

Still, it wasn't lost on me that the machine in the
game was a symbol of sorts for the computer on which
I was playing it. And then there was the long gray
cord that connected the computer to the great wide
world beyond. There, for me, was the true magic: I
could dial up and connect to something new called the
internet.

Nowadays, connectivity is just presumed. Smartphones, laptops, desktops, everything's connected, always.

Connected to what exactly? How? It doesn't matter. You just tap the icon, and boom, you've got it: the news, pizza, streaming music, and streaming video that we used to call TV and movies. Back then, however, we plugged our modems directly into the wall.

I'm not saying that I knew much about what the internet was, or how exactly I was connecting to it, but I did understand the miraculousness of it all. Because in those days, when you told the computer to connect, you were setting off an entire process. It would beep and hiss like a traffic jam of snakes, after which—and it could take whole minutes—you could pick up any other phone in the house on an extension line and actually *hear the computers talking.* You couldn't understand what they were saying to each other, of course, since they were speaking in a machine language that transmitted up to fourteen thousand symbols per second.

Internet access, and the emergence of the Web, was my generation's big bang. It irrevocably altered the course of my life, as it did the lives of everyone. The internet was my sanctuary. If it were possible, I became more sedentary. If it were possible, I became more pale. Gradually, I stopped sleeping at night and instead slept by day in school. My grades went back into free fall.

I wasn't worried by this academic setback, however, and I'm not sure that my parents were, either. After all, the education that I was getting online seemed better and even more practical for my future career prospects than anything provided by school. That, at least, was what I kept telling my mother and father.

My appetite wasn't limited to serious tech subjects like how to fix a CD-ROM drive, of course. I also spent plenty of time on gaming sites. But I was generally just so overwhelmed by the sheer amount of information immediately available that I'm not sure I was able to say where one subject ended and another began. A crash course on how to build my own computer led to a crash course in processor architecture, with side excursions into information about martial arts, guns, and sports cars.

It was like I was in a race with the technology. I started to resent my parents whenever they would force me off the computer on a school night. I couldn't bear to have those privileges revoked, disturbed by the thought that every moment that I wasn't online more and more material was appearing that I'd be missing.

How can I explain it to someone who wasn't there? Back then, being online was another life, considered by most to be separate and distinct from Real Life. The virtual and the actual had not yet merged. And it was up to each individual user to determine for themselves where one ended and the other began.

It was precisely this that was so inspiring: the freedom to imagine something entirely new, the freedom to start over. As the millennium approached, the online world became increasingly centralized and consolidated, with both governments and businesses accelerating their attempts to intervene in what had always been a fundamentally peer-to-peer relationship. But for one brief and beautiful stretch of time the internet was mostly made of, by, and for the people. Its purpose was to enlighten, not to make money. I consider the 1990s online to have been the most pleasant and successful anarchy I've ever experienced.

I was especially involved with the Web-based bulletin-board systems or BBSs. On these, you could pick a username and type out whatever message you wanted to post, either adding to a preexisting group discussion or starting a new one. Imagine the longest email chain you've ever been on, but in public. These were also chat applications, which provided an instant message version of the same experience. There you could discuss any topic in real time.

Most of the messaging and chatting I did was in search of answers to questions I had about how to build my own computer, and the responses I received were so considered and thorough, so generous and kind, they'd be unthinkable today. My panicked query about why a certain chipset for which I'd saved up my allowance didn't seem to be compatible with the motherboard I'd already gotten for Christmas received a two-thousand-word explanation from a professional tenured computer scientist on the other side of the country. I was twelve years old, and my correspondent was an adult stranger far away, yet he treated me like an equal because I'd shown respect for the technology.

I attribute this civility, so far removed from our current social media sniping, to the fact that the only people on these boards were the people who wanted to be there badly enough—who had the proficiency and passion. The internet of the 1990s wasn't just one click away. It took significant effort just to log on.

Once, a certain BBS that I was on tried to coordinate in-the-flesh meetings of its regular members throughout the country: in DC, in New York, at the Consumer Electronics Show in Las Vegas. After being pressured rather hard to attend—and promised extravagant evenings of eating and drinking—I finally told everyone how old I was. I was afraid that some of my correspondents might stop interacting with me, but instead they became, if anything, even more encouraging. I was sent updates from the electronics show and images of its catalog; one guy offered to ship me secondhand computer parts through the mail, free of charge.

•   •   •   •   •   •   •

I might have told the BBSers my age, but I never told them my name, because one of the greatest joys of these platforms was that on them I didn't have to be who I was. I could be anybody. I could take cover under virtually any handle, or "nym," as they were called, and suddenly become an older, taller, manlier version of myself. I could even be multiple selves. I took advantage of this feature by asking my more amateur questions on what seemed to me the more amateur boards under different personas each time. My computer skills were improving so swiftly that I was embarrassed by my previous ignorance and wanted to distance myself from it. I wanted to disassociate my selves.

The internet back then had yet to fall victim to the move by both governments and businesses to link users' online personas to their offline legal identity. Kids used to be able to go online and say the dumbest things one day without having to be held accountable for them the next. That scenario actually encouraged me and those of my generation to change our most deeply held opinions, instead of just digging in and defending them when challenged. This ability to reinvent ourselves meant that we never had to close our minds by picking sides. Mistakes were swiftly punished, but also swiftly rectified, and that allowed both the community and the "offender" to move on. To me, and to many, this felt like freedom. Imagine: You could wake up every morning and pick a new name and a new face by which to be known to the world, as if the internet button were actually a reset button for your life.

FIVE

Hacking

LL TEENS ARE HACKERS. THEY HAVE TO BE,
if only because their life circumstances are
untenable and they're willing to do anything to
evade parental supervision. Basically, they're fed up with
being on the losing end of an imbalance of power.

To grow up is to realize the extent to which your
existence has been governed by systems of rules, vague
guidelines, and increasingly unsupportable norms that
have been imposed on you without your consent and are
subject to change at a moment's notice.

In school, you were told that in the system of
American politics, citizens give consent through the fran-
chise to be governed by their equals. This is democracy.

But democracy certainly wasn't in place in my US history class. If my classmates and I had had the vote, Mr. Martin would have been out of a job. If a teacher didn't want you to go to the bathroom, you'd better hold it in. If a teacher promised a field trip but then canceled it for an imaginary infraction, they'd offer no explanation beyond citing their broad authority and the maintenance of proper order.

Even back then, I realized that any opposition to this system would be difficult. Getting rules changed would involve persuading the rule makers to put themselves at a disadvantage. That, ultimately, is the critical flaw in every system, in both politics and computing: The people who create the rules have no incentive to act against themselves.

So I started hacking—which remains the sanest, healthiest, and most educational way I know for anyone to assert autonomy and address people on equal terms.

Like most of my classmates, I didn't like the rules but was afraid of breaking them. I knew how the system worked: You corrected a teacher's mistake, you got a warning; you confronted the teacher when they didn't admit the mistake, you got detention; someone cheated off your exam, and though you didn't expressly let them cheat, you got detention and the cheater got suspended.

This is the origin of all hacking: the awareness of

a link between input and output, between cause and effect. Hacking isn't just native to computing—it exists wherever rules do. To hack a system requires getting to know its rules better than the people who created it or are running it, and taking advantage of the space between how those people had intended the system to work and how it actually works. In making the most of these unintentional uses, hackers aren't breaking the rules so much as debunking them. Hacking is a reliable method for dealing with the type of authority figures so convinced of their system's righteousness that it never occurred to them to test it.

I didn't learn any of this at school, of course. I learned it online. The internet gave me the chance to pursue all the topics I was interested in, and all the links between them. The more time I spent online, the more my schoolwork felt extracurricular.

The summer I turned thirteen, I resolved to seriously reduce my classroom commitments. I wasn't quite sure how I'd swing that, though. All the plans I came up with were likely to backfire. If I was caught skipping class, my parents would revoke my computer privileges; if I decided to drop out, they'd bury my body deep in the woods and tell the neighbors I'd run away. I had to come up with a hack—and then, on the first day of the new school year, I found one. Indeed, it was basically handed to me.

At the start of each class, the teachers passed out their syllabi, detailing the material to be covered, the required reading, and the schedule of tests and quizzes and assignments. Along with these, they gave us their grading policies, which were essentially explanations of how As, Bs, Cs, and Ds were calculated. I'd never encountered information like this. Their numbers and letters were like a strange equation that suggested a solution to my problem.

After school that day, I sat down with the syllabi and did the math to figure out which aspects of each class I could simply ignore and still expect to receive a passing grade. Take my US history class, for example. According to the syllabus, quizzes were worth 25 percent, tests were worth 35 percent, term papers were worth 15 percent, homework was worth 15 percent, and class participation—that most subjective of categories, in every subject—was worth 10 percent. Because I usually did well on my quizzes and tests without having to do too much studying, I could count on them for easy, time-efficient points. Term papers and homework, however, were the major time-sucks: low-value, high-cost impositions on Me Time.

If I didn't do any homework but aced everything else, I'd wind up with a cumulative grade of 85, a B. If I didn't do any homework or write any term papers but aced everything else, I'd wind up with a cumulative grade of 70, a C-minus. The 10 percent that was class participation would be my buffer. Even if the teacher gave me a zero in that, I could still manage a 65, a D-minus. I'd still pass.

My teachers' systems were terminally flawed. Their instructions for how to achieve the highest grade could be used as instructions for how to achieve the highest freedom—a key to how to avoid doing what I didn't like to do and still slide by.

The moment I figured that out, I stopped doing homework completely. Every day was bliss. Until Mr. Stockton asked me in front of the entire class why I hadn't handed in the past half dozen or so homework assignments. I cheerfully offered my equation to the math teacher.

"Pretty clever, Eddie," Mr. Stockton said, moving on to the next lesson with a smile.

I was the smartest kid in school—until about twenty-four hours later, when Mr. Stockton passed out the new syllabus. This stated that any student who failed to turn in more than six homework assignments by the end of the semester would get an automatic F.

Pretty clever, Mr. Stockton.

Then he took me aside after class and said, "You should be using that brain of yours not to figure out how to avoid work, but how to do the best work you can. You have so much potential, Ed. But I don't think you realize that the grades you get here will follow you for the rest of your life. You have to start thinking about your permanent record."

· · · · · · ·

I also did some more conventional—computer-based—hacking. As I did, my abilities improved. At the bookstore, I'd page through tiny, blurrily photocopied, stapled-together hacker zines, absorbing their techniques, and in the process absorbing their antiauthoritarian politics.

People still ask me why, when I finally did gain some hacking proficiency, I didn't race out to empty bank accounts or steal credit card numbers. The honest answer is that I was too young and dumb to even know that this was an option, let alone to know what I'd do with the stolen loot. All I wanted, all I needed, I already had for free. Instead, I figured out simple ways to hack some games, giving myself extra lives and letting me do things like see through walls. Also, there wasn't a lot of money on the internet back then, at least not by today's standards.

If you asked some of the big-shot hackers of the day why, for example, they'd hacked into a major news site only to do nothing more meaningful than replace the headlines with a goofy GIF that would be taken down in half an hour, the reply would've been a version of the answer given by the mountaineer who was asked his reason for climbing Mount Everest: "Because it's there." Most hackers, particularly young ones, set out to search for the limits of their talent and any opportunity to prove the impossible possible.

I was young, and while my curiosity was pure, it was also pretty revealing. The more I came to know about the fragility of computer security, the more I worried over the consequences of trusting the wrong machine. My first hack that ever courted trouble dealt with the fear of a full-on, scorched-earth nuclear holocaust.

I'd been reading some article about the history of the American nuclear program, and before I knew it, with just a couple of clicks, I was at the website of the Los Alamos National Laboratory, the country's nuclear research facility. That's just the way the internet works: You get curious, and your fingers do the thinking for you. But suddenly I was legitimately freaked out: The website of America's largest and most significant scientific research and weapons development institution, I noticed, had a glaring security hole. Its vulnerability was basically the virtual version of an unlocked door. Within a half hour of reading an article about the threat of nuclear weapons, I'd stumbled upon a trove of files meant only for the lab's security-cleared workers.

To be sure, the documents I accessed weren't exactly the classified plans for building a nuclear device in my garage. (And, anyway, it's not as if those plans weren't already available on about a dozen DIY websites.) Still, as someone suddenly worried about nuclear war, and also as the child of military parents, I did what I figured I was supposed to: I told an adult. I sent an explanatory email to the laboratory's webmaster about the vulnerable files and waited for a response that never came.

Every day after school I visited the site to check if it had been updated, and it hadn't—nothing had changed, except my capacity for shock and indignation. I finally called the general information phone number listed at the bottom of the laboratory's site.

An operator picked up, and the moment she did, I started stammering. She interrupted with a curt "Please hold for IT," and before I could thank her, she'd transferred me to a voice mail.

By the time the beep came, I'd regained some confidence, and I left a message. I think I even spelled out my name, like my father sometimes did, using the military phonetic alphabet: "Sierra November Oscar Whiskey Delta Echo November." Then I hung up and went on with my life, which for a week consisted pretty much exclusively of checking the Los Alamos website.

Nowadays, given the government's cyber-intelligence

capabilities, anyone who was pinging the Los Alamos servers a few dozen times a day would almost certainly become a person of interest. Back then, however, I was merely an interested person. I couldn't understand— didn't anybody care?

Weeks passed until one evening, just before dinner, the phone rang. My mother, who was in the kitchen making dinner, picked up.

I was at the computer in the dining room when I heard it was for me: "Yes, uh-huh, he's here." Then: "May I ask who's calling?"

I turned around in my seat, and she was standing over me, holding the phone against her chest. All the color had left her face. She was trembling.

Her whisper terrified me. "What did you do?"

Had I known, I would have told her. Instead, I asked, "Who is it?"

"Los Alamos, the nuclear laboratory."

"Oh, thank God."

I gently pried the phone away from her and sat her down. "Hello?"

On the line was a friendly representative from Los Alamos IT, who kept calling me Mr. Snowden. He thanked me for reporting the problem and informed me that they'd just fixed it. I restrained myself from asking what had taken so long—and from reaching over to the computer and immediately checking the site.

My mother hadn't taken her eyes off me. I gave her a thumbs-up, and then, to further reassure her, I explained to the IT rep what he already knew: how I'd found the problem, how I'd reported it, how I hadn't received any response until now. I finished up with, "I really appreciate you telling me. I hope I didn't cause any problems."

"Not at all," the IT rep said, and then asked what I did for a living.

"Nothing really," I said.

He asked whether I was looking for a job, and I said, "During the school year, I'm pretty busy, but I've got a lot of vacation and the summers are free."

That's when he realized that he was dealing with a teenager. "Well, kid," he said, "you've got my contact. Be sure and get in touch when you turn eighteen. Now pass me along to that nice lady I spoke to."

I handed the phone to my anxious mother, and she took it back with her into the kitchen, which was filling up with smoke. Dinner was burned, but I'm guessing the IT rep said enough complimentary things about me that any punishment I was imagining went out the window.

SIX

Incomplete

I DON'T REMEMBER HIGH SCHOOL VERY WELL because I'd spent so much of it asleep, compensating for all my insomniac nights on the computer. At Arundel High, most of my teachers didn't mind my little napping habit and left me alone so long as I wasn't snoring, though there were still a cruel, joyless few who considered it their duty to always wake me with a question: "And what do *you* think, Mr. Snowden?"

I'd lift my head off my desk, sit up in my chair, yawn, and—as my classmates tried to stifle their laughter—have to answer.

The truth is, I loved these moments, which were among the greatest challenges high school had to offer.

I loved being put on the spot, groggy and dazed, with thirty pairs of eyes and ears trained on me and expecting my failure while I searched for a clue on the half-empty blackboard. If I could think quickly enough to come up with a good answer, I'd be a legend. But if I was too slow, I could always crack a joke—it's never too late for a joke. In the absolute worst case, I'd sputter, and my classmates would think I was stupid. Let them. You should always let people underestimate you. Because when people mis-appraise your intelligence and abilities, they're merely pointing out their own vulnerabilities—the gaping holes in their judgment that need to stay open if you want to cartwheel through later on a flaming horse, correcting the record with your sword of justice.

At the time, I believed that life's most important questions were binary, meaning that one answer was always Right, and all the rest were Wrong. I think I was enchanted by the model of computer programming, whose questions can only be answered in one of two ways: 1 or 0, the machine-code version of yes or no, true or false. Even the multiple-choice questions of my quizzes and tests could be approached through binary logic. If I didn't immediately recognize one of the possible answers as correct, I could always try to reduce my choices by a process of elimination.

Toward the end of my freshman year, however, I was

faced with a very different kind of assignment—a question that couldn't be answered by filling in bubbles with a number-two pencil. It was an English class assignment, a writing prompt: "Please produce an autobiographical statement of no fewer than 1,000 words." I was being ordered to divulge my thoughts on perhaps the only subject on which I didn't have any thoughts: the subject of me. I just couldn't do it. I didn't turn anything in and received an incomplete.

My problem, like the prompt itself, was personal—my family was falling apart. My parents were getting a divorce. It all happened so fast. My father moved out, and my mother moved us into a condominium in a development in nearby Ellicott City. As the custody and visitation rights were being sorted, my sister threw herself into college applications.

I reacted by turning inward. Among family, I was dependable and sincere. Among friends, cheery and unconcerned. But when I was alone, I was constantly worried about being a burden. Every fuss I'd ever made flickered in my mind, evidence that I was responsible for what had happened between my parents.

I started faking self-sufficiency, projecting a sort of premature adulthood. I stopped saying that I was "playing" with the computer and started saying that I was "working" on it. Just changing those words, without remotely changing what I was doing, made a difference in how I was perceived, by others and even by myself.

I stopped calling myself Eddie. From now on, I was Ed. I got my first cell phone, which I wore clipped to my belt like a grown-up.

I was surprised to find that as I put more and more distance between myself and my parents, I became closer to others, who treated me like a peer. Mentors who taught me to sail, trained me to fight, coached me in public speaking, and gave me the confidence to stand onstage—all of them helped to raise me.

At the beginning of my sophomore year, though, I started getting tired a lot and falling asleep more than usual—not just at school anymore, but now even at the computer. Soon enough my joints were aching, my nodes were swollen, the whites of my eyes turned yellow, and I was too exhausted to get out of bed, even after sleeping for twelve hours or more at a stretch.

I was eventually diagnosed with infectious mononucleosis. It was both a seriously debilitating and seriously humiliating illness for me to have, not least because it's usually contracted through what my classmates called "hooking up," and at age fifteen the only hooking up I'd ever done involved a modem. School was totally forgotten, my absences piled up. I barely had the energy to do anything but play the games my parents gave me. When

I no longer had it in me to even work a joystick, I wondered why I was alive.

It was a haze. While I was resigned to all the fever
dreams sleep brought me, the thought of having to catch
up on my schoolwork was the true nightmare. After I'd
missed approximately four months of class, I got a letter in the mail informing me that I'd have to repeat my
sophomore year. The prospect of returning to school, let
alone of repeating two semesters, was unimaginable to
me, and I was ready to do whatever it took to avoid it.

Suddenly I was upright and getting dressed in something other than pajamas. I was online and on the
phone, searching for the system's edges, searching for
a hack. After a bit of research, and a lot of form filling,
my solution landed in the mailbox: I'd gotten myself
accepted to college. Apparently, you don't need a high
school diploma to apply.

Anne Arundel Community College wasn't a fancy
university, but it would do the trick. All that mattered
was that it was accredited. I took the offer of admission to my high school administrators, who agreed to
let me enroll. I'd attend college classes two days a week,
which was just about the most that I could manage to
stay upright and functional. By taking classes above my
grade level, I wouldn't have to suffer through the year
I'd missed. I'd just skip it.

I was the youngest person in all my classes, and might even have been the youngest person at the school. This, along with the fact that I was still recovering, meant that I didn't hang out much. Also, because AACC was a commuter school, it had no active campus life. The anonymity of the school suited me fine, though, as did my classes, most of which were distinctly more interesting than anything I'd napped through at Arundel High.

· · · · · · ·

Before I go any further, I should note that I still owe that English class autobiographical statement. The older I get, the heavier it weighs on me, and yet writing it hasn't gotten any easier.

It's hard to have spent so much of my life trying to avoid identification, only to turn around completely and share "personal disclosures" in a book. The Intelligence Community tries to instill in its workers a baseline anonymity, a sort of blank-page personality. You train yourself to be inconspicuous, to look and sound like others. You live in the most ordinary house; you drive the most ordinary car; you wear the same ordinary clothes as everyone else. The difference is, you do it on purpose: normalcy, the ordinary, is your cover.

An autobiographical statement is static, the fixed

document of a person in flux. This is why the best account that someone can ever give of themselves is not a statement but a pledge—a pledge to the principles they value and to the vision of the person they hope to become.

I'd enrolled in community college to save myself time after a setback, not because I intended to continue with my higher education. But I'd made a pledge to myself that I'd at least complete my high school degree. One weekend I drove out to a public school near Baltimore to take the last test I'd ever take for the state of Maryland: the exam for the General Education Development (GED) degree, which the US government recognizes as the standard equivalent to a high school diploma.

I remember leaving the exam feeling lighter than ever, having satisfied the two years of schooling that I still owed to the state just by taking a two-day exam. It felt like a hack, but it was more than that. It was me staying true to my word.

seven

9/11

From the age of sixteen, I was pretty much living on my own. With my mother throwing herself into her work, I often had the condo to myself. I set my own schedule, cooked my own meals, and did my own laundry. I was responsible for everything but paying the bills.

I had a white Honda Civic and drove it all over. My life became a circuit, tracing a route between home, college, and my friends, particularly a new group that I'd met in Japanese class. Most of these friends were aspiring artists and graphic designers obsessed with anime. As our friendships deepened, so, too, did my familiarity with anime genres.

One of my new friends—I'll call her Mae—was much older, at a comfortably adult twenty-five. She was something of an idol to the rest of us, as a published artist and avid cosplayer. She was my Japanese conversation partner and, I was impressed to find out, also ran a successful Web-design business.

That's how I became a freelancer: I started working as a Web designer for a girl I met in class. I was a quick learner, and in a company of two, you've got to be able to do everything. We worked out of her house, a two-story town house that she shared with her husband, a neat and clever man whom I'll call Norm.

The town house was located on base at Fort Meade, where Norm worked as an air force linguist assigned to the NSA. It's nearly inconceivable now, but at the time, Fort Meade was almost entirely accessible to anyone. It wasn't all barricades and checkpoints trapped in barbed wire like it is today. I could just drive onto the army base housing the world's most secretive intelligence agency in my '92 Civic, windows down, radio up, without having to stop at a gate and show ID.

Mae was strikingly canny, working twice as hard as her peers to make her business a success. She parlayed her illustration skills into logo design and offered basic branding services. As for my work, the methods and coding were simple enough for me to pick up on the fly, and although they could be brutally repetitive, I wasn't complaining.

Still, about a year into my job, I realized I had to plan for my future. Most job listings and contracts for advanced work were beginning to require that applicants be officially accredited by major tech companies like IBM and Cisco in the use and service of their products. The certification credentials were being adopted as industry standard almost as quickly as the industry could invent them. An A+ certification meant that you were able to service and repair computers. A Net+ certification meant that you were able to handle some basic networking. But these were just ways to become the guy who worked the help desk. The best pieces of paper were grouped under the Microsoft Certified Professional series. The most advanced certification, the Microsoft Certified Systems Engineer, or MCSE, was the brass ring, the guaranteed meal ticket.

In terms of technical know-how, the MCSE wasn't the easiest to get, but it also didn't require what most self-respecting hackers would consider unicorn genius, either. In terms of time and money, the commitment was considerable. I had to take seven separate tests, which cost 150 dollars each, and pay something like eighteen thousand dollars in tuition to Johns Hopkins University for the full battery of prep classes. True to form, I didn't finish the classes, opting instead to go straight to the testing after I felt I'd had enough. Unfortunately, Hopkins didn't give refunds. With payments looming on my tuition loan, I asked Mae to give me more hours. She agreed and told me to start coming in at 9:00 a.m. It was an early start time, especially for a freelancer, which was why I was running late on Tuesday morning, September 11, 2001.

I was speeding down Route 32 under a beautiful Microsoft-blue sky, trying not to get caught by any speed traps. My window was down, and my hand was riding the wind—it felt like a lucky day. I had the talk radio cranked and was waiting for the news to switch to the traffic.

Just as I was about to take a shortcut into Fort Meade, an update broke through about a plane crash in New York City.

When Mae came to her door, I followed her up the stairs to the cramped office next to her bedroom. There wasn't much to it: just our two desks side by side, a drawing table for her art, and a cage for her squirrels. Though I was slightly distracted by the news, we had work to do. I forced myself to focus on the task at hand. I was just opening the project's files when the phone rang.

Mae picked up. "What? Really?"

Because we were sitting so close together, I could hear her husband's voice. And he was yelling.

Mae's expression turned to alarm, and she loaded a news site on her computer. I was reading the site's report about a plane hitting one of the Twin Towers of the World Trade Center in New York City, when Mae said, "Okay. Wow. Okay," and hung up.

She turned to me. "A second plane just hit the other tower." Until that moment, I'd thought it had been an accident.

Mae said, "Norm thinks they're going to close the base."

"Like, the gates?" I said. "Seriously?"

The scale of what had happened had yet to hit me. I was thinking about my commute.

"Norm said you should go home. He doesn't want you to get stuck."

I sighed and saved the work I'd barely started. Just when I got up to leave, the phone rang again, and this time the conversation was even shorter. Mae was pale.

"You're not going to believe this."

The Pentagon, the headquarters of the Department of Defense, had been attacked.

Pandemonium, chaos: our most ancient forms of terror. For as long as I live, I'll remember retracing my way up the road past the NSA's headquarters. At the moment of the worst terrorist attack in American history, the staff of the National Security Agency was abandoning its work by the thousands, and I was swept up in the flood.

NSA director Michael Hayden issued the order to evacuate before most of the country even knew what had happened. Later, the NSA and the CIA—which also evacuated all but a skeleton crew from its own headquarters at Langley in McLean, Virginia, on 9/11—would explain the evacuations by citing a concern that one of the agencies might potentially, possibly, perhaps be the target of the fourth and last hijacked airplane, United Airlines Flight 93, rather than the White House or Capitol.

I wasn't thinking about the next likeliest targets as my car crawled through the gridlock caused by everyone trying to get out of the same parking lot simultaneously. I wasn't thinking about anything at all. What I was doing was obediently following along, in what today I recall as a clamor of horns (I don't think I'd ever heard a car horn at an American military installation before) and radios shrieking the news of the South Tower's collapse while drivers steered with their knees and feverishly pressed redial on their phones. (Calls were just about impossible to make due to an overloaded cell network.) Gradually, I realized that I was cut off from the world and stalled bumper to bumper. Even though I was in the driver's seat, I was just a passenger.

Eventually the NSA's special police went to work directing traffic. In the ensuing hours, days, and weeks, they'd be joined by convoys of Humvees topped with machine guns, guarding new roadblocks and checkpoints. Many of these new security measures became permanent, supplemented by endless rolls of wire and massive installations of surveillance cameras. With all this security, it became difficult for me to get back on base and drive past the NSA—until the day I was employed there.

EIGHT

9/12

Try to remember the biggest family event you've ever been to—maybe a family reunion. How many people were there? Around thirty, fifty? Though all of them together make up your family, you might not really have gotten the chance to know each and every individual member. Now think about how many people are in your school. How many of them are your friends, and how many others do you just know as acquaintances, and how many others do you simply recognize? It certainly stretches the boundaries of what you could say are all "your people," but you may still feel a bond with them.

Nearly three thousand people died on 9/11. The

events of that day left holes. Holes in families, holes in communities. Holes in the ground.

Now, consider this: Over one million people have been killed in the course of America's response to the attacks.

The two decades since 9/11 have seen America self-destruct by way of secret policies, secret laws, secret courts, and secret wars, whose traumatizing impact—whose very existence—the US government has repeatedly classified, denied, disclaimed, and distorted. Having spent roughly half that period as an employee of the American Intelligence Community and roughly the other half in exile, I know better than most how often the agencies get things wrong. I know, too, how intelligence can be used for disinformation and propaganda against America's enemies, but also against its allies and sometimes its own citizens. Whenever I try to understand how the last two decades happened, I return to that September—to that ground-zero day and its immediate aftermath.

I remember escaping the panicked crush of the spies fleeing Fort Meade just as the North Tower of the World Trade Center came down. Once on the highway, I tried to steer with one hand while pressing buttons with the other, calling family indiscriminately and never getting through. Finally, I managed to get in touch with my mother, who was working as a clerk for the federal courts in Baltimore.

Her voice scared me, and suddenly the only thing in the world that mattered to me was reassuring her.

"It's okay. I'm headed off base," I said. "Nobody's in New York, right?"

"I don't—I don't know. I can't get in touch with Gran."

"Is Pop in Washington?"

"He could be in the Pentagon for all I know."

The breath went out of me. By 2001, my grandfather had retired from the Coast Guard and was now a senior official in the FBI, serving as one of the heads of its aviation section. This meant that he spent plenty of time in plenty of federal buildings throughout DC.

Before I could say anything, my mother spoke again. "There's someone on the other line. It might be Gran. I've got to go."

She didn't call me back. I tried her number endlessly but couldn't get through, so I went home to wait, sitting in front of the blaring TV while I kept reloading news sites.

My mother's drive back from Baltimore was a slog through crisis traffic. She arrived in tears, but we were among the lucky ones. Pop was safe.

The next time we saw Gran and Pop, there was a lot of talk—about Christmas plans, about New Year's plans— but the Pentagon and the towers were never mentioned.

My father, by contrast, vividly recounted his 9/11 to me. He was at Coast Guard Headquarters when the

World Trade Center towers were hit, and he and three of his fellow officers found a conference room with a screen so they could watch the news coverage. A young officer rushed past them down the hall and said, "They just bombed the Pentagon." Met with expressions of disbelief, the young officer repeated, "I'm serious—they just bombed the Pentagon." My father hustled over to a wall-length window that gave him a view across the Potomac of about two-fifths of the Pentagon and swirling clouds of thick black smoke.

The more that my father related this memory, the more intrigued I became by the line *They just bombed the Pentagon*. Every time he said it, I recall thinking, *"They"? Who were "they"?*

After 9/11, America immediately divided the world into "us" and "them," and everyone was either with us or against us, as President George W. Bush remarked while the rubble was still smoldering. People in my neighborhood put up new American flags, as if to show which side they'd chosen. Others stuffed red, white, and blue Dixie cups through every chain-link fence on every overpass of every highway between my mother's home and my father's to spell out phrases like UNITED WE STAND and STAND TOGETHER NEVER FORGET.

Nearly a hundred thousand spies returned to work with the knowledge that they'd failed at their primary job, which was protecting America. They had the same anger as everybody else, but they also felt guilt. September 12 was the first day of a new era, which America faced with a unified resolve, strengthened by a revived sense of patriotism and the goodwill and sympathy of the world. In retrospect, my country could have done so much with this opportunity. It could have used this rare moment of solidarity to reinforce democratic values in the now-connected global public.

Instead, it went to war.

The greatest regret of my life is my reflexive, unquestioning support for that decision. I accepted all the claims reported by the media as facts, and I repeated them as if I were being paid to. I wanted to be a liberator. I wanted to free the oppressed. I wanted vengeance. It's humiliating to acknowledge how easy this transformation was, and how readily I welcomed it.

I wanted, I think, to be part of something. Prior to 9/11, serving in the military had seemed pointless, or just boring. Between the fall of the Berlin Wall in 1991 and the attacks of 2001, America lacked for enemies. It was the sole global superpower. There were seemingly no new frontiers to conquer or great civic problems to solve, except online. The attacks of 9/11 changed all that. Now, finally, there was a fight.

My options dismayed me, however. I thought I could

best serve my country behind a terminal, but a normal IT job seemed too comfortable and safe for this new world. I hoped I could do something like in the movies or on TV—those hacker-versus-hacker scenes, tracking enemies and thwarting their schemes. Unfortunately for me, the primary agencies that did that—the NSA, the CIA—often required a traditional college degree. The more I read online, however, the more I realized that the post-9/11 world was a world of exceptions. The agencies were growing so much and so quickly, especially on the technical side, that they'd sometimes waive the degree requirement for military veterans. It was then that I decided to join up.

After talking to recruiters from every branch, I decided to join the army, whose leadership some in my Coast Guard family had always considered the crazy uncles of the US military.

When I told my mother, she cried for days. I knew better than to tell my father, who'd already made it very clear that I'd be wasting my technical talents there. I was twenty years old; I knew what I was doing.

The day I left, I wrote my father a letter—handwritten, not typed—that explained my decision and slipped it under the front door of his apartment. It closed with a statement that still makes me wince. *I'm sorry, Dad*, I wrote, *but this is vital for my personal growth.*

NINE

X-rays

I JOINED THE ARMY BECAUSE IT WASN'T THE Coast Guard. It didn't hurt that I'd scored high enough on its entrance exams to qualify for a chance to come out of training as a Special Forces sergeant, on a track the recruiters called 18 X-ray, which was designed to boost the ranks of the small flexible units that were doing the hardest fighting in America's increasingly shadowy and disparate wars.

The 18 X-ray program was a considerable incentive; traditionally, before 9/11, I would've had to already be in the army before being given a shot at attending the Special Forces' qualification courses. The new system worked by screening prospective soldiers up front, identifying those with the highest levels of fitness, intelligence, and language-learning ability—the ones who might make the cut—and using the appeal of special training and a rapid advance in rank to enlist promising candidates.

I'd put in a couple of months of grueling runs to prepare—I was in great shape, but I always hated running—before my recruiter called to say that my paperwork had been approved: I was in; I'd made it. I was the first candidate he'd ever signed up for the program, and I could hear the pride and cheer in his voice when he told me that after training, I'd probably be made a Special Forces Communications, Engineering, or Intelligence sergeant.

Probably.

But first, I had to get through basic training at Fort Benning, Georgia.

I sat next to the same guy the whole way down there, from bus to plane to bus, Maryland to Georgia. He was enormous, a puffy bodybuilder somewhere between two and three hundred pounds. He talked nonstop, his conversation alternating between describing how he'd slap the drill sergeant in the face if he gave him any lip and recommending the steroid cycles I should take to most effectively bulk up. I don't think he took a breath until we arrived at Fort Benning's Sand Hill training area—which,

I have to say, didn't actually seem to have that much sand.

The drill sergeants greeted us with withering fury and gave us nicknames based on our initial infractions and grave mistakes, like getting off the bus wearing a brightly colored floral-patterned shirt, or having a name that could be modified slightly into something funnier. Soon I was Snowflake and my seatmate was Daisy, and all he could do was clench his jaw—nobody dared to clench a fist—and fume.

Once the drill sergeants noticed that Daisy and I were already acquainted, and that I was the lightest in the platoon—at five foot nine and 124 pounds—and he the heaviest, they decided to entertain themselves by pairing us together as often as possible. I still remember the buddy carry, an exercise where you had to carry your supposedly wounded partner the length of a football field using a number of different methods like the "neck drag," the "fireman," and the especially comedic "bridal carry." When I had to carry Daisy, you couldn't see me beneath his bulk. Daisy would get up with a laugh, drape me around his neck like a damp towel, and go skipping along like a child in the woods.

We were always dirty and always hurting, but within weeks I was in the best shape of my life. My slight build, which had seemed like a curse, soon became an advantage, because so much of what we did were body-weight exercises. Daisy couldn't climb a rope, which I scampered up like a chipmunk. He struggled to lift his incredible bulk above the bar for the bare minimum of pull-ups, while I could do twice the number with one arm. When we did the two-minute push-up tests, they stopped me early for maxing the score.

Everywhere we went, we marched—or ran. We ran constantly. Miles before mess, miles after mess, down roads and fields and around the track while the drill sergeant called the cadence. When you're running in unit formation, the cadence lulls you, filling your ears with the din of dozens of men echoing your own shouting voice and forcing your eyes to fix on the footfalls of the runner in front of you. After a while you don't think anymore—you merely count, mile after mile. I would say it was serene if it hadn't been so deadening. I would say I was at peace if I hadn't been so tired. This was precisely as the army intended. The army makes its fighters by first training the fight out of them until they're too weak to care, or to do anything besides obey.

It was only at night in the barracks that we could get some respite, which we had to earn by toeing the line in front of our bunks, reciting the Soldier's Creed, and then singing "The Star-Spangled Banner." Daisy would always forget the words. Also, he was tone-deaf.

Sometime during the third or fourth week we were out on a land navigation movement, which is when your platoon goes into the woods and treks to predetermined coordinates, clambering over boulders and wading across streams, with just a map and a compass—no GPS, no digital technology. We'd done versions of this movement before, but never in full kit, with each of us lugging a rucksack stuffed with around fifty pounds of gear. Worse still, the raw boots the army had issued me were so wide that I floated in them. I felt my toes blister even as I set out, loping across the range.

Toward the middle of the movement, I was in the lead and scrambled atop a storm-felled tree to check our bearings. After confirming that we were on track, I went to hop down, but with one foot extended I noticed the coil of a snake directly below me. Kids in North Carolina grow up being told that all snakes are deadly, and I wasn't about to start doubting it now.

So I widened the stride of my outstretched foot, once, twice, twisting for the extra distance, falling. When my feet hit the ground, some distance beyond the snake, a fire shot up my legs that was more painful than any viper bite I could imagine. A few stumbling steps, which I had to take in order to regain my balance, told me that something was wrong. I was in excruciating pain, but I couldn't stop because I was in the army, and the army was in the middle of the woods. I gathered my resolve, pushed the pain away, and just focused on maintaining a steady pace.

I managed to tough it out and finish, but the only reason was that I didn't have a choice. By the time I got back to the barracks, my legs were numb.

The next morning, I was torn from a fitful sleep by the clanking of a metal trash can being thrown down the squad bay, a wake-up call that meant someone hadn't done their job to the drill sergeant's satisfaction. I shot up automatically, swinging myself over the edge of my bunk and springing to the floor. When I landed, my legs gave way and I fell.

Meanwhile, a crowd gathered around me with laughter that turned to concern and then to silence as the drill sergeant approached. "Daisy! Get Snowflake here down to the bench."

There's a major stigma about getting injured in the army, mostly because the army is dedicated to making its soldiers feel invincible, but also because it likes to protect itself from accusations of mis-training. This is why almost all training-injury victims are treated like whiners or worse.

After he carried me down to the bench, Daisy had to go. He wasn't hurt, and those of us who were had to be kept separated. I got partnered up with a smart, handsome, former-catalog-model Captain America type who'd injured his hip about a week earlier. Neither of us felt up to talking, so we crutched along in grim silence. At the hospital I was x-rayed and told that I had bilateral tibial fractures. These are stress fractures, which can deepen with time and pressure until they crack the bones down to the marrow. The only thing I could do to help my legs heal was to get off my feet and stay off them. It was with those orders that I was dismissed from the examination room to get a ride back to the battalion.

Except I couldn't leave without my partner. He'd gone in to be x-rayed after me and hadn't returned. I assumed he was still being examined, so I waited. And waited. Hours passed. It turned out he was in surgery.

I was sent back to Fort Benning alone. If I stayed on the bench for more than three or four days, I'd be at serious risk of being "recycled"—forced to start basic training over from scratch—or, worse, of being transferred to the medical unit and sent home.

My next doctor's appointment confirmed I wasn't long for the army. After examining me and a new set of X-rays, the doctor said that I was in no condition to continue with my company. The next phase of training was airborne, and he told me, "Son, if you jump on those legs, they're going to turn into powder."

If I didn't finish the basic training cycle on time,

I'd lose my slot in 18X, which meant that I'd be reassigned according to the needs of the army. They could make me into whatever they wanted: regular infantry, a mechanic, a desk jockey, a potato peeler, or—in my greatest nightmare—doing IT at the army's help desk.

The doctor must have seen how dejected I was, because he cleared his throat and gave me a choice: I could get recycled, or he could write me a note putting me out on what was called "administrative separation." This, he explained, was a special type of severance, not characterized as either honorable or dishonorable, only available to enlistees who'd been in the services fewer than six months. It was a clean break, and could be taken care of rather quickly.

I accepted his offer.

Shortly thereafter, I was transferred to the medical unit. I signed some forms formalizing my administrative discharge and left on crutches that the army let me keep.

Ten

Cleared and In Love

I can't remember exactly when, in the midst of my convalescence, I started thinking clearly again. First the pain had to ebb away, then gradually the depression ebbed, too, and after weeks of waking to no purpose beyond watching the clock change, I slowly began paying attention to what everyone around me was telling me: I was still young, and I still had a future. I only felt that way myself, however, once I was finally able to stand upright and walk on my own.

I was ready to face the facts: If I still had the urge to serve my country, and I most certainly did, then I'd have to serve it through my head and hands—through computing. Which meant I would need a security clearance.

There are, generally speaking, three levels of security clearance. From low to high they are confidential, secret, and top secret. A top secret clearance can also be extended with a Sensitive Compartmented Information qualifier, creating the coveted TS/SCI access required by top-tier agencies like the CIA and NSA. The TS/SCI is by far the hardest access to get, but also opens the most doors. The approval process for a TS/SCI can take a year or more. All it involves is filling out some paperwork, then sitting around with your feet up and trying not to commit too many crimes while the federal government renders its verdict. The rest, after all, is out of your hands.

On paper, I was a perfect candidate. I was a kid from a service family, nearly every adult member of which had some level of clearance; I'd tried to enlist and fight for my country until an unfortunate accident had laid me low. I had no criminal record, no drug habit. My only financial debt was the student loan for my Microsoft certification, and I hadn't yet missed a payment.

None of this stopped me, of course, from being nervous.

The goal of all this background checking was not only to find out what I'd done wrong, but also to find out how I might be compromised or blackmailed. The most important thing to the Intelligence Community (IC) is not that you're 100 percent perfectly clean, because if that were the case they wouldn't hire anybody. Instead, it's that there's no dirty secret out there that you're hiding that could be used against you, and thus against the agency, by an enemy power.

This, of course, set me thinking. Nothing I could come up with would have raised even an iota of eyebrow from investigators. Still, I was worried about my chat logs and forum posts, all the supremely moronic commentary that I'd sprayed across gaming and hacker sites when I was younger. When I went back and reread the posts, I cringed. Half the things I'd said I hadn't even meant at the time, and the other half, the things I think I had meant at the time, were even worse. I'd grown up.

This might be a familiar problem for any generation that grows up online. My generation was the first to be able to discover and explore our identities almost totally unsupervised. But we gave hardly any thought to the fact that it was all being preserved forever, and that one day we might be expected to account for it.

My situation was somewhat different, however, in that most of the message boards of my day would let you delete your old posts. Using my computer science skills, I could put together one tiny little script—not even a real program—and all of my posts would be gone in under an hour. It would've been the easiest thing in the world to do. Trust me, I considered it.

But ultimately, I couldn't. Something kept preventing me. It just felt wrong. To blank my posts from the face of the earth wasn't illegal, and it wouldn't even have made me ineligible for a security clearance had anyone found out. But the prospect of doing so bothered me nonetheless. What mattered to me wasn't so much the integrity of the written record but that of my soul. I didn't want to live in a world where everyone had to pretend that they were perfect, because that was a world that had no place for me or my friends. To erase those comments would have been to erase who I was, where I was from, and how far I'd come.

I decided to leave the comments up and figure out how to live with them. We can't erase the things that shame us, or the ways we've shamed ourselves, online. All we can do is control our reactions—whether we let the past oppress us, or accept its lessons, grow, and move on.

In the midst of waiting for the clearance process to take its course, I met Lindsay Mills on an online dating site. She would go on to become my partner and the love of my life. Our first date was a continuation of our first contact online and the start of a conversation that will last as long as we will.

I told her I was worried about the upcoming polygraph, or lie detector, test required for my clearance, and she offered to practice with me. The philosophy she lived by was the perfect training: Say what you want; say who you are; never be ashamed. If they reject you, it's their problem.

I passed the test with flying colors.

As required, I had to answer the series of questions three times in total, and all three times I passed, which meant that not only had I qualified for the TS/SCI, I'd also cleared the "full scope polygraph"—the highest clearance in the land.

I was twenty-two years old, had a girlfriend I loved, and I was on top of the world.

PART TWO

ELEVEN

The System

WHEN MY COUNTRY WENT TO WAR AFTER 9/11, I answered the call. I found that the patriotism my parents had taught me was easily converted into nationalist fervor. For a time, especially in my run-up to joining the army, my sense of the world came to resemble the duality of the least sophisticated video games, where good and evil are clearly defined and unquestionable.

However, once I returned from the army and rededicated myself to computing, I gradually came to regret this simple world view. The more I developed my abilities, the more I matured and realized that the technology of communications had a chance of succeeding where the technology of violence had failed in the US's various wars in the Middle East post-9/11. Democracy could never be imposed at the point of a gun, but perhaps it could be sown by the spread of silicon and fiber.

In the early 2000s, the internet was still just barely out of its formative period, and, to my mind at least, it offered a more authentic and complete incarnation of American ideals than even America itself. A place where everyone was equal? Check. A place dedicated to life, liberty, and the pursuit of happiness? Check, check, check. Here was this wild, open new frontier that belonged to anyone bold enough to settle it, swiftly becoming colonized by governments and corporate interests that were seeking to regulate it for power and profit.

In school, I'd had to memorize the preamble to the US Constitution. Its words lodged in my brain alongside John Perry Barlow's "A Declaration of the Independence of Cyberspace":

> *We are creating a world that all may enter without privilege or prejudice accorded by race, economic power, military force, or station of birth.*
>
> *We are creating a world where anyone, anywhere may express his or her beliefs, no matter how singular, without fear of being coerced into silence or conformity.*

This internet revolution wasn't happening in history textbooks. My generation could be part of it as long as we had the technological knowledge and abilities. But in order to flourish, I had to specialize. I could have become a software developer or, as the job is more commonly called, a programmer, writing the code that makes computers work. Alternatively, I could have become a hardware or network specialist, setting up the servers in their racks and running the wires, weaving the massive fabric that connects every computer, every device, and every file. Computers and computer programs were interesting to me, and so were the networks that linked them together. But I was most intrigued by their total functioning as an overarching system.

A system is just a bunch of parts that function together as a whole, which most people are only reminded of when something breaks. In order to find what caused the system to collapse, you have to start from the point where you spotted the problem and trace the problem's effects logically through all of the system's components. Because systems work according to instructions, ultimately when there's a problem, you're searching for which rules failed, how, and why.

Over the course of my career, it became increasingly difficult for me to ask these questions about the technologies I was responsible for and not about my country.

And it became increasingly frustrating to me that I was able to repair the former but not the latter. I ended my time in Intelligence convinced that my country's operating system—its government—had decided that it functioned best when broken.

●　　●　　●　●　●　●　●　　●

I had hoped to serve my country, but instead I went to work for it. There is a difference. The sort of honorable stability offered to my father and Pop wasn't quite as available to me, or to anyone of my generation. Both my father and Pop entered the service of their country on the first day of their working lives and retired from that service on the last. That was the American government that was familiar to me. It had helped to feed, clothe, and house me. That government had treated a citizen's service like a compact: It would provide for you and your family, in return for your integrity and the prime years of your life.

But I came into the IC during a different age.

By the time I arrived, the sincerity of public service had given way to the greed of the private sector. The sacred compact of the soldier, officer, and career civil servant was being replaced by a transient worker, or contractor, whose patriotism depended on a better paycheck and for whom the federal government was less the ultimate authority than the ultimate client.

However much the work of Intelligence is privatized, the federal government remains the only authority that can grant an individual clearance to access classified information. And because clearance candidates must be sponsored in order to apply for clearance—meaning they must already have a job offer for a position that requires clearance—most Intelligence contractors begin their careers in a government position.

The government job that had sponsored me for my TS/SCI clearance wasn't the one I wanted but the one I could find: I was officially an employee of the state of Maryland, working for the University of Maryland at College Park. The university was helping the NSA open a new institution called CASL, the Center for Advanced Study of Language.

CASL's ostensible mission was to study how people learned languages and to develop computer-assisted methods to help them do so more quickly and better. The NSA also wanted to develop ways to improve computer comprehension of language. The agency was having a tough time ensuring that its computers could comprehend and analyze the massive amount of foreign-language communications that they were intercepting.

I don't have a more granular idea of the kinds of things that CASL was supposed to do for the simple reason that when I showed up for work with my bright, shiny clearance, the place wasn't even open yet. In fact, its building was still under construction. Until it was finished and the tech was installed, my job was essentially that of a night-shift security guard. My responsibilities were limited to showing up every day to patrol the empty halls making sure that nobody burned down the building or broke in and bugged it.

At the time I was still naive enough to think that my position with CASL would be a bridge to a full-time federal career. But the more I looked around, the more I was amazed to find that there were very few opportunities to serve my country directly, at least in a meaningful technical role. I had a better chance of working as a contractor for a private company that served my country for profit. And I had the best chance, it turned out, of working as a subcontractor for a private company that contracted with another private company that served my country for profit. The realization was dizzying.

It was particularly bizarre to me that most of the systems jobs that were out there were private. These positions came with almost universal access to the employer's digital existence. The US government had restructured its intelligence agencies so that its most sensitive systems were being run by somebody who didn't really work for it.

The government agencies were hiring tech companies to hire young adults from my generation, and then they were giving them the keys to the kingdom, because—as Congress and the press were told—the agencies didn't have a choice. No one else knew how the keys, or the kingdom, worked.

•   •   •   •   •   •   •

My first major contracting gig was actually a subcontracting gig: the CIA had hired BAE Systems, which had hired COMSO, which hired me.

I never learned what the company's acronym stood for, or even if it stood for anything. Technically speaking, COMSO would be my employer, but I never worked a single day at a COMSO office, or at a BAE Systems office, and few contractors ever would. I only worked at CIA headquarters.

In fact, I only ever visited the COMSO office, which was in Greenbelt, Maryland, maybe two or three times in my life. One of these was when I went down there to negotiate my salary and sign some paperwork. After the negotiations ended, a man held out his hand and, as I shook it, introduced himself to me as my "manager." He went on to explain that the title was just a formality, and that I'd be taking my orders directly from the CIA. "If all goes well," he said, "we'll never meet again."

In the spy movies and TV shows, when someone tells

you something like that, it usually means that you're about to go on a dangerous mission and might die. But in real spy life it just means "Congratulations on the job." By the time I was out the door, I'm sure he'd already forgotten my face.

TWELVE

Indoc

Y OU KNOW THAT ONE SET-UP SHOT THAT'S IN pretty much every spy movie and TV show that's subtitled *CIA Headquarters, Langley, Virginia*? And then the camera moves through the marble lobby with the wall of stars and the floor with the agency's seal? Well, Langley is the site's historical name, which the agency prefers Hollywood to use; CIA HQ is officially in McLean, Virginia; and nobody really comes through that lobby except VIPs or outsiders on a tour.

That building is the OHB, the Old Headquarters Building. The building where almost everybody who works at the CIA enters is far less glamorous: the NHB, the New Headquarters Building. My first day was one of the very few I spent there in daylight. That said, I spent most of the day underground—in a grimy, cinder block–walled room with all the charm of a nuclear fallout shelter and the acrid smell of government bleach.

"So this is the Deep State," one guy said, and almost everybody laughed. We were all computer dudes—and yes, almost uniformly dudes. Some were tattooed and pierced, or bore evidence of having removed their piercings for the big day. One still had punky streaks of dye in his hair. Almost all wore contractor badges, as green and crisp as new hundred-dollar bills.

This session was the first stage in our transformation. It was called the Indoc, or Indoctrination, and its entire point was to convince us that we were the elite, that we were special. We had been chosen to learn the mysteries of state and the truths that the rest of the country—and, at times, even its Congress and courts—couldn't handle.

Being indoctrinated into the IC, like becoming expert at technology, has powerful psychological effects. All of a sudden you have access to the story behind the story, the hidden histories of well-known, or supposedly well-known, events. Also, all of a sudden you have not just the license but the obligation to lie, conceal, and mislead. This creates a sense of tribalism, which can lead many to believe that their primary allegiance is to the institution and not to the rule of law.

I wasn't thinking any of these thoughts at my Indoc session, of course. Instead, I was just trying to keep myself awake. The presenters instructed us on basic operational security practices: Don't tell anyone who you work for. Don't leave sensitive materials unattended. Don't bring your highly insecure cell phone into the highly secure office—or talk on it about work, ever. Don't wear your *Hi, I work for the CIA* badge to the mall.

Finally, the room darkened, the PowerPoint presentation was fired up, and faces appeared on a screen. Everyone in the room sat upright. These were the faces, we were told, of former agents and contractors who had failed to follow the rules. The people on the screen, it was implied, were now in basements even worse than this one, and some would be there until they died.

All in all, this was an effective presentation.

I'm told that in the years since my career ended, this parade of horribles has been expanded to include an additional category: people of principle, whistleblowers in the public interest. I can only hope that the twentysomethings sitting there today are struck by the government's conflation of selling secrets to the enemy and disclosing them to journalists when my face pops up on the screen.

My team's task was to manage the vast majority of

the CIA servers in the continental United States—the enormous halls of expensive "big iron" computers that comprised the agency's internal networks and databases, all of its systems that transmitted, received, and stored intelligence. Many of the agency's most important servers were situated on-site. Half of them were in the NHB, where my team was located; the other half were in the nearby OHB. They were set up on opposite sides of their respective buildings, so that if one side was blown up, we wouldn't lose too many machines. My team was one of the few at the agency permitted to actually lay hands on the servers that processed and stored the agency's most important secrets. We were likely the only team with access to log in to nearly all of them.

•   •   •   •   •   •   •

After a few weeks familiarizing myself with the systems on the day shift, I moved to nights—6:00 p.m. to 6:00 a.m.—when the rest of the agency was pretty much dead.

At night, especially between, say, 10:00 p.m. and 4:00 a.m., the CIA was empty and lifeless, a vast and haunted complex with a postapocalyptic feel. All the escalators were stopped, and you had to walk them like stairs. Only half the elevators were working, and the pinging sounds they made, which were barely audible during the bustle of daytime, now sounded alarmingly loud. The agency had recently committed to a new eco-friendly energy-saving policy and installed motion-sensitive overhead lights: The lights would switch on when you approached, so that you felt followed, and your footsteps would echo endlessly.

For twelve hours each night, three days on and two days off, I sat in the secure office (or "vault," as they're called in the CIA) beyond the help desk, among the twenty desks each bearing two or three computer terminals reserved for the systems administrators who kept the CIA's global network online. Regardless of how fancy that might sound, the job itself was basically waiting for catastrophe to happen. The problems generally weren't too difficult to solve. The moment something went wrong, I had to log in to try to fix it remotely. If I couldn't, I had to physically descend into the data center hidden a floor below my own in the New Headquarters Building—or walk the eerie half mile through the connecting tunnel over to the data center in the Old Headquarters Building—and tinker around with the machinery itself.

My partner in this task—the only other person responsible for the nocturnal functioning of the CIA's entire server architecture—was a guy I'm going to call Frank. He was an exceptional personality in every sense.

He was a fiftysomething been-there-done-that ex-navy radio operator.

I have to say, when I first met Frank, I thought, *Imagine if my entire life were like the nights I spent at CASL.* Because, to put it bluntly, Frank did hardly any work at all. At least, that was the impression he liked to project. He enjoyed telling me, and everyone else, that he didn't really know anything about computing and didn't understand why they'd put him on such an important team. By his own account, all he'd done at work for the better part of the last decade was sit around and read books, though sometimes he'd also play games of solitaire—with a real deck of cards, not on the computer, of course. Sometimes he'd just pace all night.

When the phone rang to signal that something was broken, he'd just report it to the day shift. Essentially, his philosophy (if you could call it that) was that the night shift had to end sometime and the day shift had more people. Apparently, however, the day shift had gotten tired of coming in to work every morning to find Frank's feet up in front of the digital equivalent of a dumpster fire, and so I'd been hired.

For some reason, the agency had decided that it was preferable to bring me in than to let this old guy go. After a couple of weeks of working together, I was convinced that his continued employment had to be the result of some personal connection or favor. To test this hypothesis I tried to draw Frank out, but I only provoked a lecture that went on and on, until suddenly a panicked expression came over his face and he jumped up and said, "I gotta change the tape!"

I had no idea what he was talking about. But Frank was already heading to the gray door at the back of our vault, which opened onto a dingy stairwell that gave direct access to the data center itself.

Going down into a server vault—especially the CIA's—can be a disorienting experience. You descend into darkness blinking with green and red LEDs like an evil Christmas, vibrating with the whir of the industrial fans cooling the precious rack-mounted machinery to prevent it from melting down. Being there was always a bit dizzying.

Frank stopped by a shabby corner where an old computer took up almost an entire rickety desk. It was something from the early '90s or even the late '80s, a computer so ancient that it shouldn't even have been called a computer. It was more properly a *machine*, running a miniature tape format that I didn't recognize.

Next to this machine was a massive safe, which Frank unlocked.

He fussed with the tape that was in the machine, pried it free, and put it in the safe. Then he took another antique tape out of the safe and inserted it into the machine as a replacement, threading it into place. He carefully tapped a few times on the old keyboard—down, down, down, tab, tab, tab. He couldn't actually see the effect of those keystrokes, because the machine's monitor no longer worked, but he struck the enter key with confidence.

I couldn't figure out what was going on. But the itty-bitty tape began to tick-tick-tick and then spin, and Frank grinned with satisfaction.

"This is the most important machine in the building," he said. "The agency doesn't trust this digital-technology crap. They don't trust their own servers. You know they're always breaking. But when the servers break down, they risk losing what they're storing, so in order not to lose anything that comes in during the day, they back everything up on tape at night."

"So you're doing a storage backup here?"

"A storage backup to tape. The old way. Reliable as a heart attack. Tape hardly ever crashes."

It was only when Frank repeated this same tape-changing ritual the next night, and the night after that, and on every night we worked together thereafter, that I began to understand why the agency kept him around— and it wasn't just for his sense of humor. Frank was the only guy willing to stick around between 6:00 p.m. and

6:00 a.m. who was also old enough to know how to handle that proprietary tape system.

After I found a way to automate most of my own work—writing scripts to automatically update servers and restore lost network connections, mainly—I started having what I came to call a Frank amount of time. Meaning I had all night to do pretty much whatever I wanted. I passed a fair number of hours in long talks with Frank, but I also spent plenty of time online.

Few realize this, but the CIA has its own internet and Web. It has its own kind of Facebook, which allows agents to interact socially; its own type of Wikipedia, which provides agents with information about agency teams, projects, and missions; and its own internal version of Google—actually provided by Google—which allows agents to search this sprawling classified network. For hours and hours every night, this was my education. For the record, as far as I could tell, aliens have never contacted Earth, or at least they haven't contacted US intelligence.

Here is one thing that the disorganized CIA didn't quite understand at the time, and that no major American employer outside of Silicon Valley understood, either: The computer guy knows everything, or rather can know everything. The higher up this employee is, and the more systems-level privileges he has, the more access he has to virtually every byte of his employer's digital existence. Of course, not everyone is curious enough to take advantage of this education, and not everyone is possessed of a sincere curiosity. My forays through the CIA's systems were natural extensions of my childhood desire to understand how everything works, how the various components of a mechanism fit together into the whole.

With the official title and privileges of a systems administrator, and technical prowess that enabled my clearance to be used to its maximum potential, I was able to satisfy my every informational deficiency and then some. In case you were wondering: Yes, man really did land on the moon. Climate change is real. Chemtrails are not a thing.

On the CIA's internal news sites, I read top secret dispatches regarding trade talks and coups as they were still unfolding. These agency accounts of events were often very similar to the accounts that would eventually show up on network news, CNN, or Fox days later. The primary differences were merely in the sourcing and the level of detail.

Working at CIA headquarters was a thrill, but it was still only a few hours away from where I'd grown up, which in many ways was a similar environment. I was in my early twenties, and—apart from stints in North Carolina, childhood trips to visit my grandfather at

Coast Guard bases where he'd held commands, and my few weeks in the army at Fort Benning—I'd never really left the Beltway.

The excitement and significance of what I was reading both increased my appreciation of the importance of our work and made me feel like I was missing out by just sitting at a workstation. As I read about events happening in Ouagadougou, Kinshasa, and other foreign cities, I realized that I had to serve my country by doing something truly meaningful abroad. Otherwise, I thought, I'd just become a more successful Frank.

After nine months as a systems administrator, I applied for a CIA tech job abroad, and in short order I was accepted.

My last day at CIA headquarters was just a formality. I'd already done all my paperwork and traded in my green badge for a blue. All that was left to do was to sit through another indoctrination and swear an oath of loyalty—not to the government or agency that now employed me directly, but to the US Constitution. I solemnly swore to support and defend the Constitution of the United States against all enemies, foreign and domestic.

THIrTeen

The Count of the Hill

M Y FIrST orDers as a FreSHLY mInTeD officer of the government were to head for the Comfort Inn in Warrenton, Virginia, a sad, dilapidated motel whose primary client was the "State Department," by which I mean the CIA. It was the worst motel in a town of bad motels, which was probably why the CIA chose it. The Comfort Inn was to be my home for the next six months while I went to the nearby Warrenton Training Center, or, as folks there call it, the Hill.

My fellow "Innmates" and I were discouraged from telling our loved ones where we were staying and what we were doing. I leaned hard into those protocols, rarely heading back to Maryland or even talking to Lindsay on the phone. Anyway, we weren't allowed to take our phones to school, since class was classified, and we had classes all the time. Warrenton kept most of us too busy to be lonely.

The Hill serves as the heart of the CIA's field communications network, carefully located just out of nuke range from DC. The salty old techs who worked there liked to say that the CIA could survive losing its headquarters to a catastrophic attack, but it would die if it ever lost Warrenton, and now that the top of the Hill holds two enormous top secret data centers—one of which I later helped construct—I'm inclined to agree.

The Hill earned its name because of its location, which is atop, yes, a massive steepness. When I arrived, there was just one road that led in, past a purposely under-marked perimeter fence, and then up a grade so severe that whenever the temperature dropped and the road iced over, vehicles would lose traction and slide backward downhill.

Just beyond the guarded checkpoint lies the State Department's decaying diplomatic communications training facility, whose prominent location was meant to reinforce its role as cover: making the Hill appear as if it's merely a place where the American foreign service trains technologists. Beyond it, amid the back territory, were the various low, unlabeled buildings I studied in, and even farther on was the shooting range that the IC's trigger pullers used for special training. Shots would ring out in a style of firing I wasn't familiar with: *pop-pop, pop; pop-pop, pop*. A double tap meant to incapacitate, followed by an aimed shot meant to execute.

I was there as a member of class 6-06 of the BTTP, the Basic Telecommunications Training Program, whose intentionally dull name disguises one of the most classified and unusual programs in existence. Its purpose is to train TISOs (Technical Information Security Officers)— the CIA's cadre of elite "communicators," or, less formally, "commo guys." A TISO is trained to be a one-person replacement for previous generations' specialized roles of code clerk, radioman, electrician, mechanic, physical and digital security adviser, and computer technician. The main job of this undercover officer is to manage the technical infrastructure for CIA operations, most commonly overseas inside American missions, consulates, and embassies. The idea is, if you're in an American embassy, you can handle all of your technical needs internally. If you ask a local repairman to fix your secret spy base, he'll definitely do it, even for cheap, but he's also going to install hard-to-find bugs on behalf of a foreign power.

TISOs are responsible for knowing how to fix basically every machine in the building, from individual computers and computer networks to solar panels, heaters and coolers, emergency generators, satellite hookups, military encryption devices, alarms, locks, and so on. The rule is that if it plugs in or gets plugged into, it's the TISO's problem.

TISOs also have to know how to build some of these systems themselves, just as they have to know how to destroy them—when an embassy is under siege, say, after all the diplomats and most of their fellow CIA officers have been evacuated. The TISOs are always the last guys out. It's their job to send the final "off the air" message to headquarters after they've shredded, burned, wiped, and disintegrated anything that has the CIA's fingerprints on it to ensure that nothing of value remains for an enemy to capture.

TISOs work under diplomatic cover with credentials that hide them among foreign service officers, usually under the identity of "attachés." The largest embassies would have maybe five of these people, but most just have one. They're called "singletons." To be a singleton is to be the lone technical officer, far from home, in a world where everything is always broken.

My class in Warrenton began with around eight members and lost only one before graduation—which I was told was fairly uncommon. For the first time in my IC career, at age twenty-four, I wasn't the youngest in the room. Most of the others were just tech-inclined people straight out of college, or straight off the street, who'd applied online.

We called each other by nicknames more often than by our true names. My nickname—I guess I can't avoid it—was the Count because, like the vampire puppet of *Sesame Street*, I had a tendency to interrupt class by raising my forefinger, as if to say, *One, two, three, ah, ha, ha, three things you forgot!*

We'd cycle through some twenty different classes, each in its own specialty, but most having to do with how to make the technology available in any given environment serve the government of the United States, whether in an embassy or on the run.

One of Warrenton's major subjects of study involved how to service the terminals and cables, the basic components of any CIA station's communications infrastructure. A *terminal*, in this context, is just a computer used to send and receive messages over a single secure network. In the CIA, the word *cables* tends to refer to the messages themselves, but technical officers know that cables are also the cords or wires that for the last half century or so have linked the agency's terminals all over the world, tunneling underground across national borders, buried at the bottom of the ocean.

Closing in on graduation, we had to fill out what

were called dream sheets. We were given a list of the CIA stations worldwide that needed personnel and were told to rank them in the order of our preferences. These dream sheets then went to the Requirements Division, which promptly crumpled them up and tossed them in the trash—at least according to rumor.

My dream sheet started with what was called the SRD, the Special Requirements Division. This was technically a posting in Virginia, from which I would be sent out on periodic tours of places where the agency judged a permanent posting too harsh or too dangerous—tiny, isolated forward operating bases in Afghanistan, Iraq, and the border regions of Pakistan, for example. By choosing SRD, I was opting for challenge and variety over being stuck in just one city for the entire duration of what was supposed to be an up-to-three-years stint. My instructors were all pretty confident that SRD would jump at the chance to bring me on, and I was pretty confident in my newly honed abilities. But things didn't quite go as expected.

As was evident from the condition of the Comfort Inn, the school had been cutting some corners. Some of my classmates had begun to suspect that the administration was actually violating federal labor laws by requiring unpaid overtime, denying leave, and refusing to honor family benefits.

These grievances came to a head when the decrepit stairs at the Comfort Inn finally collapsed. A few of my classmates approached me. They knew that I was well liked by the instructors, since my skills put me near the top of my class. They were also aware, because I'd worked at headquarters, that I knew my way around the bureaucracy. Plus I could write pretty well—at least by tech standards. They wanted me to act as a sort of class representative, or class martyr, by formally bringing their complaints to the head of the school.

Within an hour I was compiling policies to cite from the internal network, and before the day was done my email was sent. The next morning the head of the school had me come into his office. He admitted the school had gone off the rails but said the problems weren't anything he could solve. "You're only here for twelve more weeks—do me a favor and just tell your classmates to suck it up. Assignments are coming up soon, and then you'll have better things to worry about. All you'll remember from your time here is who had the best performance review."

What he said had been worded in such a way that it might've been a threat, and it might've been a bribe. Either way, it bothered me. By the time I left his office, it was justice I was after.

I rewrote and re-sent the email—not to the head of

the school now, but to his boss, the director of Field Service Group. Then I copied the email to *his* boss.

A few days later, we were in class when a front-office secretary came in and declared that unpaid over-time would no longer be required, and, effective in two weeks, we were all being moved to a much nicer hotel. I remember the giddy pride with which she announced, "A Hampton Inn!"

I had only a day or so to revel in my glory before class was interrupted again. This time, the head of the school was at the door, summoning me back to his office. There, waiting in the school head's office, was the director of the Field Service Group—the school head's boss, the boss of nearly everyone on the TISO career track, the boss whose boss I'd emailed. He was exceptionally cordial, which unnerved me.

I tried to keep a calm exterior, but inside I was sweating. The head of the school began our chat by reiterating how the issues the class had brought to light were in the process of being resolved. His superior cut him off. "But why we're here is not to talk about that. Why we're here is to talk about insubordination and the chain of command."

If he'd slapped me, I would've been less shocked.

The CIA was quite different from the other civilian agencies, he said, even if, on paper, the regulations

insisted it wasn't. And in an agency that did such important work, there was nothing more important than the
chain of command.

I pointed out that I'd *tried* the chain of command
and been failed by it. Which was precisely the last thing
I should have been explaining to the chain of command
itself, personified just across a desk from me.

The head of the school just stared at his shoes and
occasionally glanced out the window.

"Listen," his boss said. "Ed, I'm not here to file a 'hurt
feelings report.' Relax. I recognize that you're a talented
guy, and we've gone around and talked to all of your
instructors, and they say you're talented and sharp. Even
volunteered for the war zone. That's something we appreciate. We want you here, but we need to know that we
can count on you. You've got to understand that there's
a system here. Sometimes we've all got to put up with
things we don't like because the mission comes first,
and we can't complete that mission if every guy on the
team is second-guessing." He paused, swallowed, and
said, "Nowhere is this more true than in the desert. A lot
of things happen out in the desert, and I'm not sure that
we're at a stage yet where I'm comfortable you'll know
how to handle them."

In other words, I wasn't getting the SRD posting I'd
so coveted.

This was their gotcha, their retaliation. No one besides me—and I mean no one—had put down SRD, or any other active combat situation for that matter, as their first or second or even third choice on their dream sheets. Everyone else had prioritized all sweet European vacation-stations with windmills and bicycles, where you rarely hear explosions.

Almost perversely, they now gave me one of these assignments. They gave me Geneva. They punished me by giving me what I'd never asked for, but what everybody else had wanted.

Fourteen

Geneva

Mary Shelley's *Frankenstein*, written in 1818, is largely set in Geneva, the bustling, neat, clean, clockwork-organized Swiss city where I now made my home. I read it at night during the long, lonely months I spent by myself before Lindsay moved over to join me, stretched out on a bare mattress in the living room of the comically fancy, comically vast, but still almost entirely unfurnished apartment that the embassy was paying for.

In the Intelligence Community, the "Frankenstein effect" is widely cited: situations in which decisions intended to advance American interests end up harming them irreparably. In Geneva, in the same landscape where Mary Shelley's monster ran amok, America was busy creating a network that would eventually take on a life and mission of its own and wreak havoc on the lives of its creators—mine very much included. The CIA station in the American embassy in Geneva was one of the prime European laboratories of this decades-long experiment.

The CIA is the primary American intelligence agency dedicated to HUMINT (human intelligence), or covert intelligence gathering by means of interpersonal contact—person to person, face-to-face. In other words, when you think of traditional undercover spy missions in movies, you're thinking of HUMINT (with lots of embellishment, of course). This differs from SIGINT (signals intelligence), or covert intelligence gathering by means of intercepted communications. Though the COs (case officers) who specialized in HUMINT had a general distrust of digital technology, they certainly understood how useful it could be.

To serve as a technical field officer among these people was to be as much a cultural ambassador as an expert adviser. On Monday, a CO might ask my advice on how to set up a covert online communications channel with a potential turncoat they were afraid to spook. On Tuesday, another CO might introduce me to someone they'd say was a "specialist" in from Washington—though this was

in fact the same CO from the day before, now testing out a disguise that I'm still embarrassed to say I
didn't suspect in the least, though I suppose that was
the point. On Wednesday, I might be asked how best
to destroy after transmitting (the technological version
of burn after reading) a disc of customer records that a
CO had managed to purchase from a crooked Swisscom
employee. On Thursday, I might have to write up and
transmit security violation reports on COs, documenting
minor infractions like forgetting to lock the door to a
vault when they'd gone to the bathroom. (I once had
to write up myself for exactly the same mistake.) Come
Friday, the chief of operations might call me into his
office and ask me if, "hypothetically speaking," headquarters could send over an infected thumb drive that
could be used by "someone" to hack the computers used
by delegates to the United Nations, whose main building was just up the street. Did I think there was much
of a chance of this "someone" being caught?

I didn't, and they weren't.

During my time in the field, the field was rapidly
changing. The agency was increasingly adamant that COs
enter the new millennium, and technical field officers
like myself were tasked with helping them do that in
addition to all of our other duties. We put them online,
and they put up with us.

The notoriously slow and meticulous methods of traditional spycraft certainly had their successes. But with the world's deepest secrets now stored on computers, which were more often than not connected to the open internet, it was only logical that America's intelligence agencies would want to use those very same connections to steal them.

Before the advent of the internet, if an agency wanted to gain access to a target's computer, it had to recruit a person, or what spies call an "asset," who had physical access to it. But this new world of "digital network intelligence" meant that physical access was almost never required. An agent now could just send the target a message, such as an email, with attachments or links that unleashed malware (an evil program) that would allow the agency to surveil not just the target's computer but its entire network. Given this innovation, the CIA's HUMINT would be dedicated to the identification of targets of interest, and SIGINT would take care of the rest.

That, at least, was the hope. But as intelligence increasingly became "cyberintelligence," old concerns also had to be updated to the new medium of the internet. For example: how to research a target while remaining anonymous online.

Normally when you go online, your request for any

website travels from your computer more or less directly to the server that hosts your final destination—the website you're trying to visit. At every stop along the way, however, your request cheerfully announces exactly where on the internet it came from and exactly where on the internet it's going, thanks to identifiers called source and destination headers, which you can think of as the address information on a postcard. Because of these headers, your internet browsing can easily be identified as yours by, among others, webmasters, network administrators, and foreign intelligence services.

It may be hard to believe, but the agency at the time had no good answer for what a case officer should do to remain anonymous online. Formally, the way this ridiculous procedure was supposed to work was that someone back in McLean would go online from a specific computer terminal and set up a fake origin for a query before sending it to Google. If anyone tried to look into who had run that particular search, all they would find would be a fake business located somewhere in America that the CIA used as cover. I can say with absolute certainty that the process was ineffective, onerous, and expensive.

During my stint in Geneva, whenever a CO would ask me if there was a safer, faster, and all-around more efficient way to do this, I introduced them to Tor.

Tor is free and open-source software that, if used

carefully, allows its users to browse online with the closest thing to perfect anonymity. Its protocols were developed by the US Naval Research Laboratory throughout the mid-1990s, and in 2003 it was released to the public. Tor operates on a cooperative community model, relying on tech-savvy volunteers all over the globe who run their own Tor servers out of their basements, attics, and garages.

For me, Tor was a life changer, bringing me back to the internet of my childhood by giving me just the slightest taste of freedom from being observed.

•   •   •   •   •   •   •

None of this is meant to imply that the agency wasn't still doing some significant HUMINT, in the same manner in which it had always done so. Even I got involved, though my most memorable operation was a failure. Geneva was the first and only time in my intelligence career in which I made the personal acquaintance of a "target."

I met the man at an embassy party. The embassy had lots of those. The COs always went, and sometimes they would bring me along. As a technologist, I found it incredibly easy to defend my cover. The moment someone asked me what I did, and I responded with the four words "I work in IT," their interest in me was over.

The party I'm recalling took place on a warm night on the outside terrace of an upscale café. I took my plate and sat down at a table next to a well-dressed Middle Eastern man. He seemed lonely and totally exasperated that no one seemed interested in him, so I asked him about himself. That's the usual technique: just be curious and let them talk. In this case, the man did so much talking that it was like I wasn't even there. He was Saudi and told me about how much he loved Geneva. With a touch of a conspiratorial tone, he then said that he worked in private wealth management and mentioned his clients.

"Your clients?" I asked.

That's when he said, "Most of my work is on Saudi accounts."

After a few minutes, I excused myself to go to the bathroom, and on the way there I leaned over to tell the CO what I'd learned. I passed along this information because Saudi Arabia was suspected of financing terrorism. After an intentionally long interval "fixing my hair," or texting Lindsay in front of the bathroom mirror, I returned to find the CO sitting in my chair. I waved to my new Saudi friend before sitting down at a different table. My job identifying an asset was done.

The next day, the CO, whom I'll call Cal, heaped me with praise and thanked me effusively. COs are promoted or passed over based primarily on how effective they are at recruiting assets with access to information on matters substantial enough to be formally reported back to headquarters.

Despite Cal's regular meetings with the banker, the banker wasn't warming up to him—and Cal was getting impatient. After a month of failures, Cal was so frustrated that he took the banker out and intentionally got him drunk. Then he pressured the guy to drive home drunk instead of taking a cab. Before the guy had even left the last bar of the night, Cal called the Geneva police, who not fifteen minutes later arrested the banker for driving under the influence. The banker faced an enormous fine. When the fine was levied, and his "friend" couldn't afford to pay, Cal was ready with a loan. Suddenly the banker had become dependent on him, the dream of every CO.

In the end, though, when the CO finally made the pitch to the banker to become an asset, the man turned him down. He cut off all contact and returned to Saudi Arabia. The CO was rotated back to the States. It was a waste, which I myself had put in motion and then was powerless to stop. After that experience, the prioritizing of SIGINT over HUMINT made all the more sense to me.

In the summer of 2008, the city had its annual giant carnival that culminates in fireworks. I remember sitting with the local personnel of the Special Collection Service, a joint CIA-NSA program responsible for installing and operating surveillance equipment that allows US embassies to spy on foreign signals. The work these guys did was way beyond my abilities, and they had access to NSA tools that I didn't even know existed. Still, we were friendly: I looked up to them, and they looked out for me.

As the fireworks exploded overhead, I was talking about the banker's case, lamenting the disaster it had been. One of the guys turned to me and said, "Next time you meet someone, Ed, don't bother with the COs—just give us his email address, and we'll take care of it." At the time I barely had a clue of the full implications of what that comment meant.

FIFTEEN

Tokyo

THE INTERNET IS FUNDAMENTALLY AMERICAN, but I had to leave America to fully understand what that meant. Over 90 percent of the world's internet traffic passes through technologies developed, owned, and/or operated by the American government and American businesses.

Though some of these companies might manufacture their devices in, say, China, the companies themselves are American and are subject to American law. They're also subject to classified American policies that permit the US government to surveil virtually every man, woman, and child who has ever touched a computer or picked up a phone.

It should have been obvious that the US government would engage in this type of mass surveillance. It should have been especially obvious to me. Yet it wasn't—mostly because the government kept insisting that it did nothing of the sort. All of us were too trusting. But I didn't know that until some time after I moved to Japan in 2009 to work for the NSA.

It was a dream job, not only because it was with the most advanced intelligence agency on the planet, but also because it was based in Japan, a place that had always fascinated Lindsay and me. It felt like a country from the future. Mine was officially a contractor position, and it's ironic that only by going private again was I put in a position to understand what my government was doing.

The NSA's Pacific Technical Center (PTC) occupied one half of a building inside the enormous Yokota Air Base. As the headquarters of US Forces Japan, the base was surrounded by high walls, steel gates, and guarded checkpoints. Yokota and the PTC were just a short bike ride from where Lindsay and I got an apartment in Fussa, a city at the western edge of Tokyo.

My official job title was systems analyst, with responsibility for maintaining the local NSA systems. Much of my initial work was that of a systems administrator, though, helping to connect the NSA's systems with the CIA's.

Two things about the NSA stunned me right off the bat: how technologically sophisticated it was compared with the CIA, and how much less vigilant it was about security.

It was rather disconcerting to find out that the NSA was so far ahead of the game in terms of cyberintelligence, yet so far behind it in terms of cybersecurity. My chiefs at the PTC understood the risks, so they tasked me with engineering a solution. The result was a backup and storage system: a complete, automated, and constantly updating copy of all of the agency's most important material. It allowed the agency to store intelligence data for progressively longer periods of time. The goal quickly went from being able to store intelligence for days, to weeks, to months, to five years or more. The agency's ultimate dream is permanency—to store all of the files it has ever collected or produced forever, and so create a perfect memory. The permanent record.

The NSA has a whole protocol you're supposed to follow when you give a program a code name. An internal website throws imaginary dice to pick one name from column A, and throws again to pick one name from column B. This is how you end up with names that don't mean anything, like FOXACID and EGOTISTICALGIRAFFE. But agents at the NSA would often cheat and redo their dice throws until they got the name combination they wanted, whatever they thought was cool: TRAFFICTHIEF, the VPN Attack Orchestrator.

I swear I never did that when I went about finding a name for my backup system. I swear that I just rolled the bones and came up with EPICSHELTER. Later, once the agency adopted the system, they renamed it something like the Storage Modernization Plan or Storage Modernization Program.

• • • • • • •

In the midst of my EPICSHELTER work, the PTC hosted a conference on China, and I was asked to make a presentation. To prepare, I started pulling everything off the NSA network (and off the CIA network, to which I still had access), trying to read every top secret report I could find about what the Chinese were doing online.

What I read were the technical details of China's surveillance of private communications—an accounting of the mechanisms and machinery required for the constant collection, storage, and analysis of the billions of daily telephone and internet communications of over a billion people. Essentially, China was spying on the private lives of its own citizens. At first I was so impressed by the system's achievement that I almost forgot to be appalled by its totalitarian controls.

But there were certain aspects of what I was reading

that disturbed me. I was reminded that if something can be done, it probably will be done, and possibly already has been. There was simply no way for America to have so much information about what the Chinese were doing without having done some of the very same things itself. What China was doing publicly to its own citizens, America might be—could be—doing secretly to the world.

And although you should hate me for it, I have to say that at the time I did my best to ignore my concerns. The distinctions were still fairly clear to me. China's system was intended to keep its citizens in and America out. The American systems were invisible and purely defensive. Understood this way, the US surveillance model was perfectly okay with me.

But in the sleepless days that followed, some dim suspicion still stirred in my mind. Long after I gave my China briefing, I couldn't help but keep digging around.

•　•　•　•　•　•　•

At the start of my employment with the NSA, in 2009, I was only slightly more knowledgeable about its practices than the rest of the world. I was aware of the agency's surveillance initiatives authorized by President George W. Bush in the immediate aftermath of 9/11, especially the warrantless wiretapping of the President's Surveillance Program (PSP).

The PSP empowered the NSA to collect telephone and internet communications between the United States and abroad without having to obtain a special warrant—in other words, there was no need for the NSA to prove that someone was suspected of wrongdoing in order to spy on them. That was a drastic, potentially unconstitutional change from how wiretapping had worked in the past.

The Bush administration claimed to have let the program expire in 2007. But the expiration turned out to be a farce. When Congress passed the Protect America Act of 2007 and the FISA Amendments Act of 2008, it gave the NSA approval for the warrantless collection of outbound telephone and internet communications originating within American borders.

That, at least, was the picture I got after reading the government's own summary of the situation in an unclassified report compiled by the inspectors general from five government agencies. I couldn't help but notice the fact that hardly any of the executive branch officials who had authorized these programs had agreed to be interviewed by the inspectors general. I interpreted their absence from the record as an admission of malfeasance, or wrongdoing by a public official.

My suspicions sent me searching for the classified version of the report, but such a version appeared not to exist. I didn't understand. I wondered whether I was looking in the wrong places. After a while of finding nothing, I decided to drop the issue. Life took over, and I had work to do.

It was only later, long after I'd forgotten about it, that the classified version came skimming across my desktop. Once it turned up, I realized why I hadn't had any luck finding it previously: It couldn't be seen, not even by the heads of agencies. It was filed in an Exceptionally Controlled Information (ECI) compartment, an extremely rare classification used only to make sure that something would remain hidden even from those holding top secret clearance. Because of my position, I was familiar with most of the ECIs at the NSA, but not this one.

The report came to my attention by mistake: Someone in the NSA IG's office had left a draft copy on a system that I had access to. Here was everything that was missing from the unclassified version. And the activities it outlined were so deeply criminal that no government would ever allow it to be released unredacted, or uncensored.

The classified version immediately exposed the unclassified document as an outright and carefully concocted lie. The only thing these two particular reports had in common was their title.

The classified report outlined what it called "a collection gap," and pointed to the necessity of the bulk collection of internet communications. The code name for this bulk collection initiative was STELLARWIND; it was the classified report's deepest secret. It was, in fact, the NSA's deepest secret. The program's very existence was an indication that the agency's mission had been transformed from using technology to defend America to using technology to control it.

At any time, the government could dig through the past communications of anyone it wanted to victimize in search of a crime (and everybody's communications contain evidence of something). At any point, for all perpetuity, any new administration—any future rogue head of the NSA—could just show up to work and, as easily as flicking a switch, instantly track everybody with a phone or a computer, know who they were, where they were, what they were doing with whom, and what they had ever done in the past.

●　　●　　●　　●　　●　　●　　●

The term *mass surveillance* is more clear to me, and I think to most people, than the government's preferred *bulk collection*, which to my mind threatens to give a falsely fuzzy impression of the agency's work. *Bulk collection* makes it sound like a particularly busy post office or sanitation department, as opposed to a historic effort to achieve total access to—and clandestinely take possession of—the records of all digital communications in existence.

But even once a common ground of terminology is established, misperceptions can still abound.

Most people, even today, tend to think of mass surveillance in terms of content—the actual words they use when they make a phone call or write an email. When they find out that the government actually cares comparatively little about that content, they tend to care comparatively little about government surveillance. The unfortunate truth, however, is that the content of our communications is rarely as revealing as the unwritten, unspoken information that can expose the broader context and patterns of behavior.

The NSA calls this "metadata." Metadata is data about data. It is, more accurately, data that is made by data— all the records of all the things you do on your devices and all the things your devices do on their own. Take a phone call, for example: Its metadata might include the date and time of the call, the call's duration, the number from which the call was made, the number being called, and their locations. An email's metadata might include information about what type of computer it was generated on, who the computer belonged to, who sent the email, who received it, where and when it was sent and received, and who if anyone besides the sender and recipient accessed it, and where and when.

Metadata can tell the address you slept at last night and what time you got up this morning. It reveals every place you visited during your day and how long you spent there. It shows who you were in touch with and who was in touch with you.

It's this fact that obliterates any government claim that metadata is somehow not a direct window into the substance of a communication. With the dizzying volume of digital communications in the world, there is simply no way that every phone call could be listened to or email read. Even if it were feasible, however, it still wouldn't be useful, and anyway, metadata makes this unnecessary by winnowing the field. This is why it's best to regard metadata not as some benign abstraction, but as the very essence of content: It is precisely the first line of information that the party surveilling you requires.

There's another thing, too: Content is usually defined as something that you knowingly produce. You know what you're saying during a phone call or what you're writing in an email. But you have hardly any control over the metadata you produce, because it is generated automatically. Your devices are constantly communicating for you whether you want them to or not.

After reading this classified report, I spent the next weeks, even months, in a daze. I was sad and low, trying to deny everything I was thinking and feeling—that's what was going on in my head toward the end of my stint in Japan. I felt like a fool, as someone of supposedly serious technical skills who'd somehow helped to build an essential component of this system without realizing its purpose. I felt used, as an employee of the IC who only now was realizing that all along I'd been protecting not my country but the state. I felt, above all, violated.

I realized that if my generation didn't intervene, the escalation would only continue. It would be a tragedy if, by the time we'd finally resolved to resist, such resistance were futile. The generations to come would have to get used to a world in which surveillance was a constant and indiscriminate presence: the ear that always hears, the eye that always sees, a memory that is sleepless and permanent.

sixteen

Home on the Cloud

In 2011, I was back in the states, working for Dell, but now attached to my old agency, the CIA. I'd decided it was best to live in denial and just make some money, make life better for the people I loved.

Counting Geneva, and not counting periodic trips home, I'd been away for nearly four years. The America I returned to felt like a changed country. Every other conversation was about some TV show or movie I didn't know, or a celebrity scandal I didn't care about, and I couldn't respond—I had nothing to respond with. A normal life was what Lindsay and I were hoping for. We were ready for the next stage and had decided to settle down. Lindsay was getting certified as a yoga instructor. I, meanwhile, was getting used to my new position—in sales.

My main project was to help the CIA by building it a "private cloud." It felt as if every major tech company, including Dell, was rolling out new civilian versions of what I was working on. I was amazed at how willingly people were signing up, so excited at the prospect of their photos and videos and music and e-books being universally backed up and available that they never gave much thought as to why such an über-sophisticated and convenient storage solution was being offered to them for "free" or for "cheap" in the first place.

I don't think I'd ever seen such a concept be so uniformly bought into. I wondered what the point was of my getting so worked up over government surveillance if my friends, neighbors, and fellow citizens were more than happy to invite corporate surveillance into their homes. It would still be another half decade before virtual assistants like Amazon Echo and Google Home were placed proudly on nightstands to record and transmit all activity within range, to log all habits and preferences, which would then be developed into advertising algorithms and converted into cash.

From the standpoint of a regular user, a cloud is just a storage mechanism that ensures that your data is being processed or stored not on your personal device, but on a range of different servers, which can ultimately be owned and operated by different companies. The result is that your data is no longer truly yours. It's controlled by companies, which can use it for virtually any purpose.

When we choose to store our data online, we're often ceding our claim to it. Companies can delete any data they object to. Unless we've kept a separate copy on our own machines or drives, this data will be lost to us forever. If any of our data is found to be in violation of the terms of service, the companies can delete our accounts, deny us our own data, and yet retain a copy for their own records, which they can turn over to the authorities without our knowledge or consent. Ultimately, the privacy of our data depends on the ownership of our data. There is no property less protected, and yet no property more private.

•　　•　　•　　•　　•　　•　　•

The internet I'd grown up with was disappearing. The very act of going online, which had once seemed like a marvelous adventure, now seemed like a fraught ordeal. Every transaction was a potential danger.

The majority of American internet users lived their entire digital lives on email, social media, and e-commerce platforms owned by Google, Facebook, and Amazon. The

American IC was seeking to take advantage of that fact by obtaining access to their networks—both through direct orders that were kept secret from the public, and clandestine efforts that were kept secret from the companies themselves. Our user data was turning vast profits for the companies, and the government pilfered it for free. I don't think I'd ever felt so powerless.

Every morning when I left our town house, I found myself nodding at the security cameras dotted throughout our development. Previously I'd never paid them any attention, but now, when a light turned red on my commute, I couldn't help but think of its leering sensor, keeping tabs on me. License-plate readers were recording my comings and goings, even if I maintained a speed of thirty-five miles per hour.

In the American system of democracy, law enforcement is expected to protect citizens from one another. In turn, the courts are expected to restrain that power when it's abused. Law enforcement is prohibited from surveilling private citizens on their property and taking possession of their private recordings without a warrant. There are few laws, however, that restrain the surveillance of public property, which includes the vast majority of America's streets and sidewalks.

Law enforcement's use of surveillance cameras on public property was originally conceived of as a crime deterrent and an aid to investigators after a crime had occurred. But as the cost of these devices continued to fall, law enforcement began using them to track people who had not committed, or were not even suspected of, any crime. And the greatest danger still lies ahead, with the refinement of artificial intelligence capabilities such as facial and pattern recognition. An AI-equipped sur-veillance camera could be made into a sort of automated police officer—a true robocop. Even in 2011, it was clear to me that this was where technology was leading us.

I began to picture a world in which all people were totally surveilled, and all laws were totally enforced, auto-matically, by computers. Such a world of total automated law enforcement would be intolerable. Most of our lives, even if we don't realize it, occur not in black and white but in a gray area, where we jaywalk, put trash in the recycling bin and recyclables in the trash, ride our bicy-cles in the improper lane, or borrow a stranger's Wi-Fi to download a book that we didn't pay for. Put simply, a world in which every law is always enforced would be a world in which everyone is a criminal.

I tried to talk to Lindsay about all this. But though she was generally sympathetic, she wasn't ready to go off the grid, or even off Facebook or Instagram. She thought I was too tense, and under too much stress. I was—not because of my work, but because of my desire to tell her a truth that I wasn't allowed to. I couldn't tell her that my former coworkers at the NSA could target her for surveillance or access all the photos she took. I couldn't tell her that her information was being collected, that everyone's information was being collected.

I began having strange physical symptoms. I'd become weirdly clumsy, falling off ladders—more than once—or bumping into door frames. Sometimes I'd trip or drop spoons I was holding. I'd spill water over myself or choke on it.

One day when I went to meet Lindsay, I started feeling dizzy. It scared me and scared Lindsay, too. I decided to go to the doctor, but the only appointment wasn't for weeks.

A day or so later, I was home around noon, trying my best to keep up with work remotely. I was on the phone with a security officer at Dell when the dizziness hit me hard. I immediately excused myself from the call, slurring my words, and as I struggled to hang up the phone, I was sure: I was going to die.

I passed out.

I came to still seated, with the clock on my desk reading just shy of 1:00 p.m. I'd been out less than an hour, but I was exhausted. I reached for the phone in a panic, but my hand kept missing it and grabbing the air. Once I managed to grab ahold of it and get a dial tone, I found I couldn't remember Lindsay's number, or could only remember the digits but not their order.

Somehow I managed to get myself downstairs, taking

each step deliberately, palm against the wall. I got some juice out of the fridge and chugged it, keeping both hands on the carton and dribbling a fair amount on my chin. Then I lay down on the floor, pressed my cheek to the cool linoleum, and fell asleep, which was how Lindsay found me.

I'd just had an epileptic seizure.

My mother had epilepsy, and I couldn't believe I hadn't associated my symptoms with hers. She'd always told me and my sister that epilepsy wasn't hereditary, meaning passed down from your parents or grandparents, and to this day I'm still not sure if that's what her doctor had told her or if she was just trying to reassure us that her fate wouldn't be ours.

Very little is known about epilepsy. I consulted as many specialists as I could find. I had CAT scans, MRIs, the works. Meanwhile, Lindsay went about researching all the information that was available about the syndrome. She googled treatments so intensely that basically all her Gmail ads were for epilepsy pharmaceuticals.

I felt defeated. First my country and the internet had betrayed me. And now my body was following suit.

My brain had, quite literally, short-circuited.

seventeen

On the Couch

T WAS LATE AT NIGHT ON MAY 1, 2011, WHEN I
noticed the news alert on my phone: Osama bin
Laden had been tracked down and killed by a
team of Navy SEALs.

So there it was. The man who'd masterminded the
attacks of September 11, 2001, who had propelled me into
the army and from there into the Intelligence Community,
was now dead.

Ten years. That's how long it had been since those
two planes had flown into the Twin Towers, and what
did we have to show for it? What had the last decade
actually accomplished? The previous ten years had been
a parade of American-made tragedy: the forever war in

Afghanistan, catastrophic regime change in Iraq, indefinite detentions of foreign prisoners at Guantánamo Bay, torture, and targeted killings of civilians—even of American civilians—via drone strikes. In America, through laws like the Patriot Act, we witnessed the steady erosion of civil liberties, the very liberties we were allegedly fighting to protect. The cumulative damage was staggering and felt entirely irreversible.

I couldn't shake the idea that I'd wasted the last decade of my life.

The biggest terrorist attack on American soil happened at the same time as the development of digital technology. Terrorism, of course, was the stated reason why most of my country's surveillance programs were implemented. The politics of terror became more powerful than the terror itself.

After a decade of mass surveillance, the technology had proved itself to be a potent weapon against liberty. By continuing these programs, by continuing these lies, which were revealed to be largely ineffective tools to stop terrorism, America was protecting little, winning nothing, and losing much.

• • • • • • •

The latter half of 2011 passed in a succession of seizures and in countless doctors' offices and hospitals. I was imaged, tested, and prescribed medications that stabilized my body but clouded my mind, turning me depressed, lethargic, and unable to focus.

I finally took a short-term disability leave from Dell and decamped to my mother's secondhand couch. I don't remember what books I tried to read, but I do remember never managing much more than a page before closing my eyes and sinking back again into the cushions. I couldn't concentrate on anything except my own weakness. Often, I was motionless but for a lone finger atop the screen of the phone that was the only light in the room.

I'd scroll through the news, then nap, then scroll again, then nap. I primarily followed protesters across the Middle East during what came to be known as the Arab Spring. Across the region, people were living under the constant threat of violence, with work and school suspended, and had no electricity, no sewage. In many regions, they didn't have access to even the most rudimentary medical care.

The crowds were calling for an end to oppression and censorship. They were declaring that in a truly just society, the people were not answerable to the government—the government was answerable to the people. They were rejecting authoritarianism.

In an authoritarian state, rights derive from the state

and are granted to the people. In a free state, rights derive from the people and are granted to the state. Though democracy has fallen far short of its ideal, I still believe it to be the one form of governance that most fully enables people of different backgrounds to live together, equal before the law.

This equality consists not only of rights but also of freedoms, including privacy. Saying that you don't need or want privacy because you have nothing to hide is to assume that no one should have, or could have, to hide anything—including their immigration status, unemployment history, financial history, and health records. Ultimately, saying that you don't care about privacy because you have nothing to hide is no different from saying you don't care about freedom of speech because you have nothing to say. Or that you don't care about freedom of the press because you don't like to read. Or that you don't care about freedom of religion because you don't believe in God. Just because this or that freedom might not have meaning to you today doesn't mean that it doesn't or won't have meaning tomorrow, to you, or to your neighbor.

The young people of the Middle East were agitating for higher wages, lower prices, and better pensions. I couldn't give them any of that. They were, however, also agitating for a freer internet.

Ever since I'd been introduced to the Tor Project in Geneva, I'd used its browser and run my own Tor server, wanting to do my professional work from home and my personal Web browsing unmonitored. Now I propelled myself off the couch and staggered over to my home office. I set up a bridge relay that would bypass the blockades the Iranian government was employing to stop its people from freely using the internet. I then distributed its encrypted configuration identity to the Tor core developers.

This was the least I could do. If there was just the slightest chance that even one young kid from Iran could now bypass the imposed filters and restrictions and connect through me online, protected by the Tor system and my server's anonymity, then it was certainly worth my minimal effort.

I imagined this person reading their email or checking their social media accounts to make sure that their friends and family had not been arrested. I had no way of knowing whether this was what they did, or whether anyone at all linked to my server from Iran. And that was the point: The aid I offered was private.

PART THREE

EIGHTEEN

Heartbeat

Imagine you're entering a tunnel. As you look down the length that stretches ahead of you, notice how the walls seem to narrow to the tiny dot of light at the other end.

My tunnel was a literal tunnel: an enormous Pearl Harbor–era airplane factory turned NSA facility located under a pineapple field in Kunia, on the island of Oahu, Hawaii. Its official name was the Kunia Regional Security Operations Center.

Lindsay and I had come to Hawaii to start over. To start over yet again.

My doctors had told me that the climate and more relaxed lifestyle in Hawaii might be beneficial for my epilepsy, since lack of sleep was thought to be the leading trigger of the seizures. Also, the move eliminated the driving problem—Maryland law prevented people diagnosed with epilepsy from driving, but Hawaiian law did not. Besides, the tunnel was a pleasant, twenty-minute bike ride to work through sugarcane fields in brilliant sunshine.

I went to work for the NSA early in 2012. The job I'd taken was a significant step down the career ladder, with duties I could at this point perform in my sleep. It was supposed to mean less stress, a lighter burden. I spent the earliest days automating my tasks—writing scripts to do my work for me—so as to free up my time for something more interesting.

Before I go any further, I want to emphasize this: My active searching out of NSA abuses began not with the copying of documents, but with the reading of them. My initial intention was just to confirm the suspicions that I'd first had back in 2009 in Tokyo. Three years later, I was determined to find out if an American system of mass surveillance existed and, if it did, how it functioned. Though I was uncertain about how to conduct this investigation, I was at least sure of this: I had to understand exactly how the system worked before I could decide what, if anything, to do about it.

I wanted to know what the NSA's surveillance

capabilities were exactly, whether and how they extended beyond the agency's actual surveillance activities, who approved them, who knew about them, and, last but surely not least, how these systems—both technical and institutional—really operated.

Sometimes I'd find a program with a recognizable name but without an explanation of what it did. Other times I'd just find a nameless explanation, with no indication as to whether the capability it described was an active program or an aspirational desire. I was running up against programs within programs. This was the nature of the NSA—by design, the left hand rarely knew what the right hand was doing.

I'm not saying that I made any decisions at that instant. The most important decisions in life are never made that way. They're made only once you're finally strong enough to admit to yourself that this is what your conscience has already chosen for you, this is the course that your beliefs have decreed. That was my twenty-ninth birthday present to myself: the awareness that I had entered a tunnel that would narrow my life down toward a single, still-indistinct act.

•　　•　　•　　•　　•　　•　　•

I got in the regular habit of perusing what the NSA called "readboards." These are digital bulletin boards that function something like news blogs, featuring the day's most important and interesting documents—everything an employee has to read to keep current.

My new, low-pressure position gave me as much time to read as I wanted. The scope of my curiosity might have raised a few questions at a prior stage of my career, but now I was the only employee of the Office of Information Sharing. I *was* the Office of Information Sharing. So my very job was to know what sharable information was out there.

In the hopes of organizing all the documents I wanted to read, I put together a best-of-the-readboards queue. The files quickly began to pile up, until the nice lady who managed the digital storage quotas complained to me about the folder size. Not wanting to erase it or stop adding to it, I decided instead to share it with others. This was the best justification for what I was doing that I could think of, especially because it allowed me to more or less legitimately collect material from a wider range of sources. So, with my boss's approval, I set about creating an automated readboard—one that edited itself.

Like EPICSHELTER, my automated readboard platform was designed to perpetually scan for new and unique documents in the networks of the NSA, the CIA, and the FBI, as well as others. The idea was that its findings would be made available to every NSA officer. Essentially, it would be a readboard of readboards. It would be run from a server that I alone managed, located just down the hall from me. That server would also store a copy of every document it sourced, making it easy for me to perform the kind of deep interagency searches that the heads of most agencies could only dream of.

I called this system Heartbeat, because it took the pulse of the NSA and of the wider IC. It pulled so many more documents than any human ever could that it immediately became the NSAnet's most comprehensive readboard.

Early on in its operation I got an email that almost stopped Heartbeat forever. A faraway administrator—apparently the only one in the entire IC who actually bothered to look at his access logs—wanted to know why a system in Hawaii was copying, one by one, every record in his database. He had immediately blocked me, which effectively locked me out, and was demanding an explanation. I told him what I was doing and showed him how to use the internal website that would let him read Heartbeat for himself. Once I gave him access, his wariness instantly turned into curiosity. He could now see that Heartbeat was just doing what it'd been meant to do and was doing it perfectly. He was fascinated. He unblocked me from his repository of records and even offered to help me by circulating information about Heartbeat to his colleagues.

Nearly all of the secret documents that I later disclosed to journalists came to me through Heartbeat. It showed me not just the aims but the abilities of the IC's mass surveillance system. This is something I want to emphasize: In mid-2012, I was just trying to get a handle on how mass surveillance actually worked. The better you can understand a program's mechanics, the better you can understand its potential for abuse.

This meant that I wasn't much interested in the briefing materials—like, for example, what has become perhaps the best-known file I disclosed. It was a slide deck from a 2011 PowerPoint presentation that explained the NSA's new surveillance approach: "Sniff It All, Know It All, Collect It All, Process It All, Exploit It All, Partner It All." This was just marketing jargon intended to impress America's allies: Australia, Canada, New Zealand, and the UK, the primary countries with which the United States shares intelligence. Together with the United States, these countries are known as the Five Eyes.

"Sniff It All" meant finding a data source; "Know It All" meant finding out what that data was; "Collect It All" meant capturing that data; "Process It All" meant analyzing that data for usable intelligence; "Exploit It All" meant using that intelligence to further the agency's aims; and "Partner It All" meant sharing the new data source with allies. But this document gave me no insight into how the approach was realized technologically.

Much more revealing was a top secret legal demand I found for a private company to turn over its customers' private information to the federal government. The order made it clear that the NSA had secretly interpreted part of the Patriot Act to mean it could collect all of the metadata coming through American telecoms such as Verizon and AT&T on "an ongoing daily basis." This included, of course, records of telephone communications between American citizens. That was unconstitutional.

I also found evidence of the NSA using other laws to justify its two most prominent internet surveillance methods: the PRISM program and upstream collection. PRISM enabled the NSA to routinely collect data from Microsoft, Yahoo!, Google, Facebook, and more, including email, photos, video and audio chats, Web-browsing content, search engine queries, and all other data stored on their clouds. Upstream collection, meanwhile, enabled direct collection of data from internet infrastructure—the switches and routers that shunt internet traffic worldwide. Together, PRISM and upstream collection ensured that the world's information, both stored and in transit, was surveillable.

The next stage of my investigation was to figure out how this collection was actually accomplished. As I came to realize, the tools behind upstream collection are the most invasive elements of the NSA's mass surveillance system.

Imagine sitting at a computer, about to visit a website. You open a Web browser, type in a URL, and hit enter. The URL is, in effect, a request, and this request goes out in search of its destination server. Before your request gets to that server, though, it will have to pass through one of the NSA's most powerful weapons.

Specifically, your request passes through a few black servers. These servers contain two critical tools. One handles making copies of the data coming through. The second is in charge of "active collection."

If the NSA finds any suspicious metadata—a particular email address, credit card, or phone number, or just certain keywords such as *protest*—then your request is diverted to the NSA's servers. There, algorithms decide which of the agency's digital weapons—malware programs— to use against you. Then the malware is delivered to you along with whatever website you requested. The end result: You get all the content you want, along with all the surveillance you don't. It all happens in less than 686 milliseconds. Completely unbeknownst to you. Now the NSA can access not just your metadata, but your data as well. Your entire digital life belongs to them.

NINETEEN

Whistleblowing

THE NSA'S surveillance programs, its domestic surveillance programs in particular, flouted the Constitution's Fourth Amendment—the one that protects us from unreasonable search and seizure—completely. The agency was essentially making a claim that the amendment's protections didn't apply to modern-day lives. The agency's internal policies neither regarded your data as your legally protected personal property nor regarded their collection of that data as a "search" or "seizure." Instead, the NSA maintained that because you had already "shared" your phone records with a "third party"—your telephone service provider— you had forfeited any constitutional privacy interest you may once have had. And it insisted that "search" and "seizure" occurred only when its analysts, not its algorithms, actively queried what had already been automatically collected.

This extremist interpretation of the Fourth Amendment—effectively, that the very act of using modern technologies means surrendering your privacy rights—would have been rejected by Congress and the courts if constitutional oversight mechanisms had been functioning properly. But when it came to protecting the privacy of American citizens in the digital age, each of the three branches of US government failed in its own way, causing the entire system to halt and catch fire. The executive branch was the primary cause of this constitutional breach. The president's office had secretly authorized mass surveillance in the wake of 9/11.

It was time to face the fact that the IC believed themselves above the law, and given how broken the process was, they were right. The IC had come to understand the rules of our system better than the people who had created it, and they used that knowledge to their advantage.

They'd hacked the Constitution.

•　　•　　•　　•　　•　　•　　•

America was born from an act of treason. The Declaration of Independence was an outrageous violation of the laws of England and yet the fullest expression of what the Founders called the "Laws of Nature," which included the right to rebel on point of principle. America's first whistleblower protection law was enacted on July 30, 1778. This law declared it "the duty of all persons in the service of the United States, as well as all other inhabitants thereof, to give the earliest information to Congress or any other proper authority of any misconduct, frauds, or misdemeanors committed by any officers or persons in the service of these states, which may come to their knowledge."

The law gave me hope—and it still does. Even at the darkest hour of the Revolution, with the very existence of the country at stake, Congress didn't just welcome an act of principled dissent, it enshrined such acts as duties. By the latter half of 2012, I was resolved to perform this duty myself. In my case, going up "the chain of command," which the IC prefers to call "the proper channels," wasn't an option. My superiors were not only aware of what the agency was doing, they were actively directing it—they were complicit.

Coming from a Coast Guard family, I've always been fascinated by how much of the English language vocabulary of disclosure has a nautical undercurrent. Organizations, like ships, sprang leaks. When steam replaced wind for propulsion, whistles were blown at sea to signal intentions and emergencies: one whistle to pass by port, two whistles to pass by starboard, five for a warning.

Ultimately, every language, including English, demonstrates its culture's relationship to power by how it chooses to define the act of disclosure. When an institution decries "a leak," it is implying that the "leaker" damaged or sabotaged something.

Today, *leaking* and *whistleblowing* are often treated as interchangeable. But to my mind, the term *leaking* should be used differently than it commonly is. It should be used to describe acts of disclosure done not out of public interest but out of self-interest. To be more precise, I understand a leak as the selective release of protected information in order to sway popular opinion or affect the course of decision making. The US government has forgiven "unauthorized" leaks when they've resulted in unexpected benefits and forgotten "authorized" leaks when they've caused harm.

A *whistleblower*, in my definition, is a person who, through hard experience, has concluded that their life inside an institution has become incompatible with the principles developed in the greater society outside it, to which that institution should be accountable. This person knows that they can't remain inside the institution and knows that the institution can't or won't be dismantled. Reforming the institution might be possible, however, so they blow the whistle and disclose the information to bring public pressure to bear.

My situation had one crucial addition: All the information I intended to disclose was classified top secret. To blow the whistle on secret programs, I'd also have to blow the whistle on the larger system of secrecy. Without bringing to light the full scope of this systemic secrecy, there would be no hope of restoring a balance of power between citizens and their government. Restoration is an essential motive of whistleblowing: The disclosure is not a radical act of dissent or resistance, but a return—signaling the ship to sail back to port.

I was resolved to bring to light a single, all-encompassing fact: that my government had developed and deployed a global system of mass surveillance without the knowledge or consent of its citizenry. The only response appropriate to the scale of the crime was a total exposure of the total apparatus of mass surveillance—not by me, but by the media, protected by the Bill of Rights.

Technologists seeking to report on the misuse of technology must do more than just bring their findings to the public. They have a duty to contextualize and explain—to demystify. A few dozen or so of the people best positioned to do this in the whole entire world were sitting all around me in the Tunnel. My fellow technologists came in every day and sat at their terminals and furthered the work of the state. They weren't merely oblivious to its abuses but incurious about them, and that lack of curiosity made them not evil but tragic. It didn't matter why they'd come to the IC: Once they'd gotten inside the machine, they became machines themselves.

TWENTY

Fourth Estate

NOTHING IS HARDER THAN LIVING WITH a secret that can't be spoken. Lying to strangers about a cover identity or concealing the fact that your office is under the world's most top secret pineapple field might sound like it qualifies, but at least you're part of a team: Though your work may be secret, it's a shared secret, and therefore a shared burden. There is misery but also laughter.

When you have a real secret, though, that you can't share with anyone, even the laughter is a lie. I could talk about my concerns, but never about where they were leading me. To the day I die I'll remember explaining to my colleagues how our work was being applied to violate the oaths we had sworn to uphold, and their response: "What can you do about it?"

I hated that question, its sense of resignation, its sense of defeat, but it still felt valid enough that I had to ask myself, *Well, what?*

When the answer presented itself, I decided to become a whistleblower. Yet to breathe to Lindsay, the love of my life, even a word about that decision would have put our relationship to an even crueler test than saying nothing. Not wishing to cause her any more harm than I was already resigned to causing, I kept silent, and in my silence I was alone.

I thought that solitude and isolation would be easy for me. Hadn't each step of my life served as a kind of preparation? Hadn't I gotten used to being alone after all those years spent in front of a screen? But I was human, too, and the lack of companionship was hard. I had everything I'd ever wanted—love, family, and success far beyond what I ever deserved. The easiest thing should have been to follow the rules.

And even if I was already reconciled to my decision—to risk everything to expose the truth—and the dangers that came with it, I wasn't yet adjusted to the role. After all, who was I to put this information in front of the American public? Who'd elected me the president of secrets?

The information I intended to disclose about my country's secret regime of mass surveillance was so explosive, and yet so technical, that I was as scared of being doubted as I was of being misunderstood. That was why my first decision, after resolving to go public, was to go public with the agency's actual files—as many as necessary to expose the scope of the abuse, though I knew that disclosing even one PDF would be enough to earn me prison.

It was clear to me that some person or institution had to vouch for the documents. Cooperating with some type of media organization would defend me against the worst accusations of rogue activity and correct for whatever biases I had. I didn't want any political opinion of mine to prejudice anything.

Lindsay had spent years patiently instilling in me the lesson that my interests and concerns weren't always hers. That just because I shared my knowledge didn't mean that anyone had to share my opinion. Not everybody who was opposed to invasions of privacy might be ready to drop off the internet entirely. Lindsay was my key to unlocking this truth—that diverse motives and approaches can only improve the chances of achieving common goals. She, without even knowing it, gave me the confidence to reach out to other people.

But which people? Who? I knew that the story the NSA documents told about a global system of mass surveillance deployed in the deepest secrecy was a difficult one to understand. It was a story so tangled and technical that I was increasingly convinced it could not be presented all at once in a "document dump." Journalists, preferably from multiple independent press institutions, needed to carefully and patiently review everything.

I knew at least two things about the members of the press: They competed for scoops, and they knew very little about technology. It was this lack of expertise or even interest in tech that largely caused journalists to miss two events that had stunned me during the course of my fact gathering about mass surveillance.

The first was the NSA's announcement of the construction of a vast new data facility in Bluffdale, Utah. The facility was projected to contain a total of four twenty-five-thousand-square-foot halls, filled with servers. It could hold an immense amount of data. The only prominent journalist who seemed to notice the announcement was James Bamford, who wrote about it for *Wired* in March 2012. But no one asked what, to me, were the most basic questions: Why does any government agency, let alone an intelligence agency, need that much space? What data, and how much of it, do they really intend to store there, and for how long? Because there was simply no reason to build something like that unless you were planning on storing absolutely everything, forever.

The second event happened one year later, in March 2013—no so-called mainstream publication covered a rare public appearance by Ira "Gus" Hunt, the chief technology officer of the CIA. The CIA had finally decided to sign a ten-year, 600-million-dollar cloud development and management deal with Amazon. So I made sure to catch Gus's appearance, because I was curious whether he might offer any insight into why Amazon had been chosen.

I got insight, certainly, but of an unexpected kind. I had the opportunity to witness the highest-ranking technical officer at the CIA brief a crowd about the agency's ambitions and capacities.

"At the CIA," he said, "we fundamentally try to collect everything and hang on to it forever." As if that wasn't clear enough, he went on: "It is nearly within our grasp to compute on <u>all</u> human generated information." The underline was Gus's own.

Gus would later explain to the journalists in the room that the agency could track their smartphones, even when they were turned off—that the agency could surveil every single one of their communications. He said, "Technology . . . is moving faster than government or law can keep up. It's moving faster . . . than you can keep up: You should be asking the question of what are your rights and who owns your data."

The lesson I took from this was that for my disclosures to be effective, I had to do more than just hand some journalists some documents. I had to become their partner, to provide the technological training and tools to help them do their reporting accurately and safely.

That would mean committing one of the capital crimes of intelligence work: I would be aiding and abetting an act of journalism. American law makes no distinction between providing classified information to the press in the public interest and providing it, even selling it, to the enemy.

Given the risks I was taking, I needed to identify people I could trust who were also trusted by the public. Above all, I had to be sure that whoever I picked wouldn't ultimately cave to power when put under pressure.

One journalist, one publication, even one country of publication wouldn't be enough. Ideally, I'd give each journalist their own set of documents simultaneously, leaving me with none. This would shift the focus of scrutiny to them and ensure that even if I were arrested, the truth would still get out.

As I narrowed down my list of potential partners, I realized my best options would be journalists whom the national security state had already targeted.

Laura Poitras I knew as a documentarian, primarily concerned with America's post-9/11 foreign policy. She had been frequently harassed by the government because of her work, repeatedly detained and interrogated by border agents whenever she traveled in or out of the country.

Glenn Greenwald I knew as a columnist for the

US edition of the British *Guardian* newspaper. I liked him because he was skeptical and argumentative. Ewen MacAskill of the British edition of the *Guardian* and Bart Gellman of the *Washington Post* would also later prove steadfast partners (and patient guides to the journalistic wilderness).

The only hitch was getting in touch.

Unable to reveal my true name, I contacted the journalists under a variety of identities. The first of these was Cincinnatus, after a legendary farmer who became a Roman consul and then voluntarily relinquished his power. The final name I used was Verax, Latin for "speaker of truth."

You can't really appreciate how hard it is to stay anonymous online until you've tried to operate as if your life depended on it. To communicate with the journalists, I decided to use somebody else's internet connection. I wish that were simply a matter of going to a McDonald's or Starbucks and signing on to their Wi-Fi. But those places have security cameras and receipts and other people. Moreover, every wireless device, from a phone to a laptop, has a globally unique identifier called a MAC (Machine Address Code), which it leaves on record with every access point it connects to.

So I didn't go to McDonald's or Starbucks—I went driving. A high-powered antenna, a magnetic GPS sensor, and a laptop allowed me to turn my car into a roving Wi-Fi sensor.

At nights and on weekends, I drove around what seemed like the entire island of Oahu, letting my antenna pick up the pulses of each Wi-Fi network. My GPS sensor tagged each access point. What resulted was a map of the invisible networks we pass by every day without even noticing.

With this network map in hand, I'd drive around Oahu like a madman, trying to check my email to see which of the journalists had replied. Some of the journalists I'd chosen needed convincing to use a more secure method of communication known as encrypted email, which back in 2012 was a pain. In some cases, I had to show them how, so I'd upload tutorials.

Atop the parking garage of a mall, secure in the knowledge that the moment I closed the lid of my laptop, my secret was safe, I'd draft manifestos explaining why I'd gone public, but then delete them. And then I'd try writing emails to Lindsay, only to delete them, too. I just couldn't find the words.

TWENTY-ONE

Read, Write, Execute

Read, write, execute: in computing, these are called permissions. The right to *read* a file allows you to access its contents, while the right to *write* a file allows you to modify it. *Execution*, meanwhile, means that you have the ability to run a file or program, to carry out the actions it was designed to do.

Read, write, execute: This was my simple three-step plan. I wanted to burrow into the heart of the world's most secure network to find the truth, make a copy of it, and get it out into the world. And I had to do all this without getting caught—without being read, written, and executed myself.

Almost everything you do on a computer, on any

device, leaves a record. Nowhere is this more true than at the NSA. Each log-in and log-out creates a log entry. Each permission I used left its own forensic trace. Every time I opened a file, every time I copied a file, that action was recorded. Every time I downloaded, moved, or deleted a file, that was recorded, too.

I used Heartbeat to compile the documents I wanted. The agency's security tools kept track of who read what, but it didn't matter: Anyone who bothered to check their logs was used to seeing Heartbeat by now. It would sound no alarms. It was the perfect cover.

While Heartbeat would work as a way of collecting the files—far too many files—it only brought them to the server in Hawaii, a server that kept logs even I couldn't get around. I needed a way to work with the files so I could discard the irrelevant and uninteresting, along with those containing legitimate secrets that I wouldn't be giving to journalists. But if I ran my searches on the Heartbeat server, it would light a massive electronic sign blinking ARREST ME.

I thought about this for a while. I couldn't just copy the files directly from the Heartbeat server onto a personal storage device and waltz out of the Tunnel without being caught. What I could do, though, was bring the files closer, directing them to an intermediate way station.

In a forgotten corner of the office was a pyramid of disused desktop computers that the agency had wiped clean and discarded. They were Dell PCs from 2009 or 2010, large gray rectangles that could store and process data on their own without being connected to the cloud. Though they were still in the NSA system, they couldn't really be closely tracked as long as I kept them off the central networks.

I could easily justify needing to use these stolid, reliable boxes by claiming that I was trying to make sure Heartbeat worked with older operating systems. Under the guise of compatibility testing, I could transfer the files to these old computers, where I could search, filter, and organize them as much as I wanted, as long as I was careful. I was carrying one of the big old hulks back to my desk when I passed one of the IT directors, who stopped me and asked me what I needed it for.

"Stealing secrets," I answered, and we laughed.

The first phase of my three-step plan ended with the files I wanted all neatly organized into folders. But they were still on a computer that wasn't mine, which was still in the Tunnel underground. Enter, then, the write phase, which for my purposes meant the agonizingly slow, scary process of copying the files onto something that I could spirit out of the building.

The easiest and safest way to copy a file off any IC

workstation is also the oldest: a camera. Smartphones, of course, are banned in NSA buildings, but workers accidentally bring them in all the time without anyone noticing. They leave them in their gym bags or in the pockets of their windbreakers. But getting a smartphone loaded with NSA secrets out of the Tunnel is risky. Odds are that nobody would've noticed—or cared—if I walked out with a smartphone, and it might have been an adequate tool for trying to copy a single report. But I wasn't wild about the idea of taking thousands of pictures of my computer screen in the middle of a top secret facility. Also, the phone would have to be configured in such a way that even the world's foremost forensic experts could seize and search it without finding anything on it that they shouldn't.

I'm going to refrain from publishing how exactly I went about my own copying and encryption (a means of securing files, which I'll explain in greater detail later on)—so that the NSA will still be standing tomorrow. I will mention, however, what storage technology I used for the copied files. Forget thumb drives; they're too bulky for the relatively small amount they store. I went, instead, for SD cards—the acronym stands for Secure Digital. Actually, I went for the mini- and micro-SD cards.

You'll recognize SD cards if you've ever used a digital

camera or video camera, or needed more storage on a tablet. They're tiny little buggers, basically the size of your pinkie fingernail—eminently concealable. You can fit one inside the pried-off square of a Rubik's Cube, then stick the square back on, and nobody will notice. In other attempts, I carried a card in my sock or, at my most paranoid, in my cheek, so I could swallow it if I had to. Eventually, as I gained confidence, and certainty in my methods of encryption, I'd just keep a card at the bottom of my pocket. They hardly ever triggered metal detectors, and who wouldn't believe I'd simply forgotten something so small?

The size of SD cards, however, has one downside: They're extremely slow. Copying times for massive volumes of data are always long—at least always longer than you want. And the duration stretches even more when you're copying to a minuscule silicon wafer embedded in plastic. Also, I wasn't just copying. I was deduplicating, compressing, and encrypting, none of which could be accomplished simultaneously. I was using all the skills I'd ever acquired in my storage work, making an off-site backup of evidence of the IC's abuses.

It could take eight hours or more—entire shifts—to fill a card. And though I switched to working nights again, those hours were terrifying. There was the old computer chugging, monitor off. And there I was, turning the monitor back on every once in a while to check the rate of progress and cringing. You know the feeling— following the completion bar as it indicates 84 percent completed, 85 percent completed . . . 1:58:53 left . . . As it filled toward the sweet relief of 100 percent, all files copied, I'd be sweating, seeing shadows and hearing footsteps around every corner.

●　　●　　●　　●　　●　　●　　●

Execute: That was the third and final step. As each card filled, I had to run my getaway routine. I had to get them out of the building, past the bosses and military uniforms, down the stairs and out the empty hall, past the badge scans and armed guards and two-doored security zones in which the next door doesn't open until the previous door shuts. And if anything goes awry, the guards draw their weapons and the doors lock you in and you say, *Well, isn't this embarrassing?* This—per all the reports I'd been studying, and all the nightmares I'd been having—was where they'd catch me; I was sure of it. Each time I left, I was petrified. I'd have to force myself not to think about the SD card. When you think about it, you act differently, suspiciously.

One unexpected upshot of gaining a better understanding of NSA surveillance was that I'd also gained a better understanding of the dangers I faced. In other words, learning about the agency's systems had taught me how not to get caught by them. The FBI—the agency that investigates all crime within the IC—took great pride in explaining exactly how they caught their suspects, and believe me, I didn't mind benefiting from their experience. It seemed that in almost every case, the FBI would wait to make its arrest until the suspect had finished their work and was about to go home. Sometimes they would let the suspect take the material out into public, where its very presence was a federal crime. I kept imagining a team of FBI agents lying in wait for me—there, out in the public light, just at the far end of the Tunnel.

I'd usually try to banter with the guards, and this was where my Rubik's Cube came in most handy. I was known to the guards and to everybody else at the Tunnel as the Rubik's Cube guy, because I was always working the cube as I walked down the halls. I got so adept I could even solve it one-handed. It became a distraction device as much for myself as for my coworkers. Most of them thought it was an affectation, or a nerdy conversation starter. And it was, but primarily it relieved my anxiety. It calmed me.

I bought a few cubes and handed them out. Anyone who took to it, I'd give them pointers. The more that people got used to them, the less they'd ever want a closer look at mine.

I got along with the guards, or I told myself I did, mostly because I knew where their minds were: elsewhere. I'd done something like their job before, back at CASL. I knew how mind-numbing it was to spend all night standing, feigning vigilance. Your feet hurt. After a while, all the rest of you hurts. And you can get so lonely that you'll talk to a wall.

I aimed to be more entertaining than the wall. There was the one guard I talked to about insomnia and the difficulties of day-sleeping (remember, I was on nights, so this would've been around two in the morning). Another guy, we discussed politics. What they all had in common was a reaction to my Rubik's Cube: It made them smile. Over the course of my employment at the Tunnel, pretty much all the guards said some variation of, "Oh man, I used to play with that when I was a kid," and then, invariably, "I tried to take the stickers off to solve it." Me too, buddy. Me too.

It was only once I got home that I was able to relax, even just slightly. I was still worried about the house being wired—that was another one of those charming methods the FBI used against those it suspected of inadequate loyalty. Lindsay would go to bed, and I'd go to the couch, hiding with my laptop under a blanket because cotton beats cameras. With the threat of immediate arrest out of the way, I could focus on transferring the files to a larger external storage device via my laptop—only somebody who didn't understand technology very well would think I'd keep them on the laptop forever. Then I'd lock them down under multiple layers of encryption algorithms using differing implementations, so that even if one failed the others would keep them safe.

I'd been careful not to leave any traces at my work and to make sure my encryption left no traces of the documents at home. Still, I knew the documents could lead back to me once I'd sent them to the journalists and they'd been decrypted. Any investigator looking at which agency employees had accessed, or could access, all these materials would come up with a list with probably only a single name on it: mine. The fact was that every individual file left me vulnerable, because all digital files contain metadata, invisible tags that can be used to identify their origins.

I struggled with how to handle this metadata situation. I worried that if I didn't strip the identifying information from the documents, they might incriminate me the moment the journalists decrypted and opened them. But I also worried that by thoroughly stripping the metadata, I risked altering the files. And if they were changed in any way, that could cast doubt on their authenticity. Which was more important: personal safety, or the public good? It might sound like an easy choice, but it took me quite a while before I owned the risk and left the metadata intact.

I was forced, for the first time, to confront the prospect of discarding my lifetime practice of anonymity and coming forward to identify myself as the source. I would embrace my principles by signing my name to them and let myself be condemned.

Altogether, the documents I selected fit on a single drive, which I left out in the open on my desk at home. I knew that the materials were just as secure now as they had ever been at the office. Actually, they were more secure, thanks to the multiple levels and methods of encryption. That's the incomparable beauty of the cryptological art, the basis of encryption. A little bit of math can accomplish what all the guns and barbed wire can't; a little bit of math can keep a secret.

TWENTY-TWO

Encrypt

MOST PEOPLE WHO USE COMPUTERS THINK there's a fourth basic permission besides read, write, and execute called delete.

Delete is everywhere on the user side of computing. It's in the hardware as a key on the keyboard, and it's in the software as an option that can be chosen from a drop-down menu. There's a certain finality that comes with choosing delete, and a certain sense of responsibility. Sometimes a box even pops up to double-check: *Are you sure?* If the computer is second-guessing you by requiring confirmation—click *Yes*—it makes sense that delete would be a major decision.

Delete functions appeared from the very start of

digital computing. Engineers understood that some choices would inevitably turn out to be mistakes. Users, regardless of whether or not they were really in control at the technical level, had to *feel* in control. If they made a file, they should be able to unmake it at will. The ability to destroy what they created and start over afresh imparted a sense of agency to the user.

Think about the reasons that you yourself press delete. On your personal computer, you might want to get rid of some document or some file you downloaded but no longer need—or some file you don't want anyone to know you ever needed. On your phone, you might delete some of the pictures, videos, and private records it automatically uploaded to the cloud. In every instance, you delete, and the thing—the file—appears to be gone.

The truth, though, is that deletion has never existed technologically in the way that we conceive of it. Deletion is a figment, a public fiction, a lie that computing tells you to reassure you and give you comfort. Although the deleted file disappears from view, it is rarely gone. In technical terms, deletion is really just a form of the middle permission, a kind of write. Normally, when you press delete for one of your files, its data—which has been stashed deep down on a disk somewhere—is not actually touched. Instead, only the computer's map of where each file is stored is rewritten to say *I'm no longer using this space for anything important*. The supposedly erased file can still be read by anyone who looks hard enough for it.

This can be confirmed through experience, actually. Next time you copy a file, ask yourself why it takes so long compared with the instantaneous act of deletion. The answer is that deletion doesn't really do anything to a file besides conceal it. Put simply, computers were not designed to correct mistakes, but to hide them—and to hide them only from those parties who don't know where to look.

•   •   •   •   •   •   •

The waning days of 2012 brought grim news: The governments of both Australia and the UK were proposing legislation for the mandatory recording of telephone and internet metadata. This was the first time that democratic governments publicly confirmed the ambition to establish a sort of surveillance time machine. Though these laws were justified as public safety measures, they represented a breathtaking intrusion into the daily lives of the innocent.

These public initiatives of mass surveillance proved, once and for all, that there could be no natural alliance between technology and government. The rift between my two strangely interrelated communities, the American IC and the global online tribe of technologists, became pretty much definitive. For years I had been able to fool myself that we were all, ultimately, on the same side of history: We were all trying to protect the internet, to keep it free for speech and free of fear. But now the government, my employer, was definitively the adversary. What my technologist peers had always suspected, I'd only recently confirmed, and I couldn't tell them. Or I couldn't tell them yet.

What I could do, however, was help them out. This was how I found myself in Honolulu as one of the hosts and teachers of a CryptoParty. This was a new type of gathering where technologists volunteered their time to teach free classes to the public on the topic of digital self-defense—essentially, showing anyone who was interested how to protect the security of their communications. I jumped at the chance to participate.

Though this might strike you as a dangerous thing for me to have done, given the other activities I was involved with at the time, it should instead just reaffirm how much faith I had in the encryption methods I taught. These were the very methods that protected that drive full of IC abuses sitting back at my house, with locks that couldn't be cracked even by the NSA. I knew that no number of documents, and no amount of journalism, would ever be enough to address the threat the world was facing. People needed tools to protect themselves, and they needed to know how to use them. Given that I was also trying to provide these tools to journalists, I was worried that my approach had become too technical. After so many sessions spent lecturing colleagues, this opportunity to simplify my subject for a general audience would benefit me as much as anyone. Also, I honestly missed teaching, which I had done often in years prior: It had been a year since I'd stood at the front of a class, and the moment I was back in that position, I realized I'd been teaching the right things to the wrong people all along.

The CryptoParty was held in a one-room art gallery behind a furniture store and coworking space. While I was setting up the projector so I could share slides showing how easy it was to run a Tor server, my students drifted in, a diverse crew of strangers and a few new friends I'd only met online. All in all, I'd say about twenty people showed up that December night to learn from me and my co-lecturer, Runa Sandvik, a bright young Norwegian woman from the Tor Project. (Runa would go on to work as the senior director of information security for the *New York Times*, which would sponsor her later CryptoParties.) Our audience wanted to re-establish a sense of control over the private spaces in their lives.

I began my presentation by discussing deletion and

the fact that total erasure could never be accomplished. The crowd understood this instantly. I went on to explain that, at best, the data they wanted no one to see couldn't be unwritten so much as overwritten: scribbled over, in a sense, until the original was rendered unreadable. But, I cautioned, even this approach had its drawbacks. There was always a chance that their operating system had silently hidden away a copy of the file they were hoping to delete in some temporary storage nook they weren't privy to.

That's when I pivoted to encryption.

Encryption is the only true protection against surveillance. If the whole of your storage drive is encrypted to begin with, your adversaries can't rummage through it for deleted files—or for anything else—unless they have the encryption key. If all the emails in your inbox are encrypted, Google can't read them to profile you— unless they have the encryption key. If all your communications that pass through hostile networks are encrypted, spies can't read them—unless they have the encryption key.

Encryption works, I explained, by way of algorithms. It's a mathematical method of transforming information— such as your emails, phone calls, photos, videos, and files—in such a way that it becomes incomprehensible to anyone who doesn't have a copy of the encryption key.

And it's reversible. You can think of a modern encryption algorithm as a magic wand that you can wave over a document to change each letter into a language that only you and those you trust can read. The encryption key is the magic spell that puts the wand to work. It doesn't matter how many people know that you used the wand, so long as you can keep your personal magic spell from anyone you don't trust.

Encryption algorithms are basically just sets of math problems designed to be incredibly difficult even for computers to solve. If all of our data, including our communications, were encrypted, then no government would be able to understand them. It could still intercept and collect the signals, but it would be intercepting and collecting pure noise. Encrypting our communications would essentially delete them from the memories of every entity we deal with. It would effectively withdraw permission from those to whom it was never granted to begin with.

Any government hoping to access encrypted communications has only two options: It can either go after the keymasters or go after the keys. The best means we have for keeping our keys safe is called "zero knowledge," a method that ensures that any data you try to store externally—say, for instance, on a company's cloud platform—is encrypted by an algorithm running on your device before it is uploaded. With zero knowledge, the key is never shared and remains in the users' hands— and only in the users' hands. No company, no agency, no enemy can touch them.

My key to the NSA's secrets went beyond zero knowledge: It was a zero-knowledge key consisting of multiple zero-knowledge keys.

My keys to the drive were hidden everywhere. But I retained one for myself. And if I destroyed that single lone piece that I kept on my person, I would destroy all access to the NSA's secrets forever.

TWENTY-THREE

The Boy

I was more curious than ever about the one fact I was still finding elusive: the absolute limit of who the IC could turn its gaze against.

The only way to discover the answer was to narrow my vision to that of the NSA employees with the freest access to the rawest forms of intelligence. They could type into their computers the names of individuals who'd fallen under the agency's suspicion, foreigners and US citizens alike. The NSA was interested in finding out everything about these individuals and their communications.

The program that enabled this access was called XKEYSCORE, which is perhaps best understood as a search engine. Imagine a kind of Google that instead of showing pages from the public internet returns results from your private email, your private chats, your private files, everything. Though I'd read enough about the program to understand how it worked, I hadn't yet used it. But I was looking for a personal confirmation of the depths of the NSA's surveillance intrusions—the kind of confirmation you don't get from documents but only from direct experience.

One of the few offices in Hawaii with truly unfettered access to XKEYSCORE was the National Threat Operations Center. As luck would have it, NTOC had a position open through a contractor job as an infrastructure analyst. The role involved using the complete spectrum of the NSA's mass surveillance tools, including XKEYSCORE.

I'd decided to bring my archives out of the country and pass them to the journalists I'd contacted, but before I could even begin to contemplate the logistics of that act I had to go shake some hands. I had to fly east to DC and spend a few weeks meeting and greeting my new bosses and colleagues. This was what brought me back home to the Beltway for the very last time, and back to Fort Meade.

The NSA described XKEYSCORE, in the documents I'd later pass on to journalists, as its "widest-ranging" tool, used to search "nearly everything a user does on the internet." It was, simply put, the closest thing to science fiction I've ever seen in science fact: an interface that allows you to type in pretty much anyone's address, telephone number, or IP address, and then basically go through the recent history of their online activity. In some cases you could even play back recordings of their online sessions, so that the screen you'd be looking at was their screen, whatever was on their desktop. You could read their emails, their browser history, their search history, their social media postings, everything. You could set up notifications that would pop up when some person or some device you were interested in became active on the internet for the day.

My weeks at Fort Meade, and the short stint I put in at my new job back in Hawaii, were the only times I saw, firsthand, the abuses actually being committed. I didn't type the names of the agency director or the president into XKEYSCORE, but after enough time with the system I realized I could have. Everyone's communications were in there—everyone's. I was initially fearful that if I searched those in the uppermost echelons of state, I'd be caught and fired, or worse.

But it was simple to disguise a query by encoding my search terms. If any of the auditors who were responsible for reviewing the searches ever bothered to look more closely, they would see only a snippet of obfuscated code, while I would be able to scroll through the most personal activities of a Supreme Court justice or a congressperson.

One thing you come to understand very quickly while using XKEYSCORE is that nearly everyone in the world who's online stores photos and videos of their family. This was true for virtually everyone of every gender, ethnicity, race, and age—from the meanest terrorist to the nicest senior citizen, who might be the meanest terrorist's grandparent or parent or cousin.

It's the family stuff that got to me the most. I remember this one child in particular, a little boy in Indonesia. Technically, I shouldn't have been interested in this little boy, but I was, because my employers were interested in his father.

The boy's father, like my own father, was an engineer—but unlike my father, this guy wasn't government or military affiliated. He was just a regular academic who'd been caught up in a surveillance dragnet. I can't even remember how or why he'd come to the agency's attention, beyond sending a job application to a research university in Iran. The grounds for suspicion were often poorly documented, if they were documented at all, and the connections could be incredibly tenuous—"believed to be potentially associated with."

Selections from the man's communications had been assembled into folders—here was the fatal copy of the résumé sent to the suspect university; here were his texts; here was his Web browser history; here was the last week or so of his correspondence both sent and received, tagged to IP addresses. Here were the coordinates of a "geo-fence" the analyst had placed around him to track whether he strayed too far from home, or perhaps traveled to the university for his interview.

Then there were his pictures, and a video. He was sitting in front of his computer, as I was sitting in front of mine. Except that in his lap he had a toddler, a boy in a diaper.

The father was trying to read something, but the kid kept shifting around, smacking the keys and giggling. The computer's internal mic picked up his giggling and there I was, listening to it on my headphones. The father held the boy tighter, and the boy straightened up and, with his dark crescent eyes, looked directly into the computer's camera—I couldn't escape the feeling that he was looking directly at me. Suddenly I realized that I'd been holding my breath. I shut the session, got up from the computer, and left the office for the bathroom in the hall, head down, headphones still on with the cord trailing.

Everything about that kid, everything about his father, reminded me of my own father, whom I met for dinner one evening during my stint at Fort Meade. I hadn't seen him in a while, but there in the midst of dinner, over bites of Caesar salad and a pink lemonade, I had the thought: *I'll never see my family again.* I knew that if I told him what I was about to do, he would've called the cops. Or else he would've called me crazy and had me committed to a mental hospital. He would've done anything he thought he had to do to prevent me from making the gravest of mistakes.

I could only hope that his hurt would in time be healed by pride.

Back in Hawaii between March and May 2013, a sense of finality hung over nearly every experience for me. It was far less painful to think that this was the last time I'd ever stop at the curry place in Mililani or drop by the art-gallery hacker space in Honolulu or just sit on the roof of my car and scan the nighttime sky for falling stars than to think that I only had another month left with Lindsay.

The preparations I was making were those of a man about to die. I emptied my bank accounts, putting cash into an old steel ammo box for Lindsay to find so that the government couldn't seize it. I went around the house doing oft-procrastinated chores, like fixing windows and changing light bulbs. I erased and encrypted my old computers. I was putting my affairs in order to try to make everything easier for Lindsay, or just for my conscience.

And yet there were moments when it seemed that the plan I'd developed was collapsing. It was difficult to get the journalists to commit to a meeting, mostly because I couldn't tell them who they were meeting with, or even, for a while at least, where and when it was happening. I had to reckon with the prospect of them never showing up, or of them showing up but then dropping out. Ultimately, I decided that if either of those happened, I'd just abandon the plan and return to work and to Lindsay as if everything were normal, to wait for my next chance.

During my Wi-Fi scavenger hunt drives I'd been researching various countries, trying to find a location for my meeting with the journalists. It felt like I was picking out my prison, or rather my grave. All of the Five Eyes countries were obviously off-limits. In fact, all of Europe was out, as were Africa and Latin America, because for various political reasons, I knew I wouldn't be safe from the American government's wrath if I got caught there. Russia was out because it was Russia, and China was China: Both were totally out of bounds. Due to the US government's contentious relationship with both countries, I knew that I'd be painted as a traitor if I settled in either country.

The process of elimination left me with Hong Kong. In geopolitical terms, it was the closest I could get to no-man's-land, but with a vibrant media and protest culture, not to mention largely unfiltered internet. In a situation with no promise of safety, it was enough to have the guarantee of time. Chances were that things weren't going to end well for me, anyway: The best I could hope for was getting the disclosures out before I was caught.

The last morning I woke up with Lindsay—she was leaving on a camping trip to Kauai with friends—I told her how sorry I was for how busy I'd been and that I was going to miss her. And that she was the best person I'd ever met in my life. She smiled, pecked me on the cheek, and then got up to pack.

The moment she was out the door, I started crying, for the first time in years.

At least I had the benefit of knowing what was coming. Lindsay would return from her camping trip to find me gone, ostensibly on a work assignment, and my mother basically waiting on our doorstep. I'd invited my mother to visit, in a move so uncharacteristic that she must have expected another type of surprise—like an announcement that Lindsay and I were engaged. I felt horrible about the false pretenses, but I kept telling myself I was justified. My mother would take care of

Lindsay, and Lindsay would take care of her. Each would need the other's strength to weather the coming storm.

The day after Lindsay left, I took an emergency medical leave of absence from work, citing epilepsy, and packed scant luggage and four laptops: secure communications, normal communications, a decoy, and an "air gap" (a computer that had never gone and would never go online). I left my smartphone on the kitchen counter alongside a notepad on which I scribbled in pen *Got called away for work. I love you.* Then I went to the airport and bought a ticket in cash for the next flight to Tokyo. In Tokyo, I bought another ticket in cash, and on May 20 arrived in Hong Kong, the city where the world first met me.

TWENTY-FOUR

Hong Kong

THE DEEP APPEAL OF GAMES, WHICH ARE really just a series of increasingly difficult challenges, is the belief that they can be won. Nowhere is this more clear to me than in the case of the Rubik's Cube. It satisfies a fantasy that if you just work hard enough and twist yourself through all of the possibilities, everything in the world that appears scrambled and incoherent will finally click into position and become perfectly aligned.

I'd had a plan—I'd had multiple plans—in which a single mistake would have meant getting caught, and yet I hadn't been: I'd made it out of the NSA; I'd made it out of the country. I had beaten the game. By every standard I could imagine, the hard part was over.

But my imagination hadn't been good enough, because the journalists I'd asked to come meet me weren't showing up. They kept postponing, giving excuses, apologizing.

I knew that Laura Poitras—to whom I'd already sent a few documents and the promise of many more—was ready to fly anywhere from New York City at a moment's notice, but she wasn't going to come alone. She was busy trying to get Glenn Greenwald to commit, trying to get him to buy a new laptop that he wouldn't put online. Trying to get him to install encryption programs so we could better communicate. And there I was, in Hong Kong, watching the clock tick away the hours, watching the calendar tick off the days. I was begging: *Please come before the NSA realizes I've been gone from work too long.* It was tough to face the prospect of being left in Hong Kong high and dry. I thought about my family and Lindsay and how foolish it was to have put my life in the hands of people who didn't even know my name.

I barricaded myself in my room at the Mira Hotel, which I chose because of its central location in a crowded shopping and business district. I put the PRIVACY PLEASE—DO NOT DISTURB sign on the door handle to keep housekeeping out. For ten days, I didn't leave the room for fear of giving a foreign spy the chance to sneak in and bug the place. With the stakes so high, the only move I had was to wait. I sent increasingly shrill pleas to my contacts. Then I'd stand at the window hoping for a reply, looking out onto the beautiful park I'd never visit. By the time Laura and Glenn finally arrived, I'd eaten every item on the room service menu.

That isn't to say that I just sat around during that week and a half writing messages. I also tried to organize the last briefing I'd ever give—going through the archive, figuring out the most effective way to explain its contents to the journalists in the surely limited time we'd have together. It was an interesting problem: how best to express to nontechnical people who were inclined to be skeptical of me that the US government was surveilling the world and the methods by which it was doing so. I put together dictionaries of terms like *metadata*. I put together glossaries of acronyms and abbreviations.

I had to find a way to help Laura and Glenn understand something in the span of a few days that it had taken me years to puzzle out. Then there was another thing: I had to help them understand who I was and why I'd decided to do this.

•   •   •   •   •   •   •

At long last, Glenn and Laura showed up in Hong Kong on June 2. When they came to meet me at the Mira, I think I disappointed them, at least initially. They even told me as much, or Glenn did: He didn't understand how a person as young as I was—he kept asking me my age—not only had access to such sensitive documents, but was also so willing to throw his life away. For my part, I didn't know how they could have expected someone older, given my instructions about how to meet: Go to a certain quiet alcove by the hotel restaurant, furnished with a pleather couch, and wait around for a guy holding a Rubik's Cube. The funny thing was that I'd originally been wary of using that bit of tradecraft, but the cube was the only thing I'd brought with me that was likely to be unique and identifiable from a distance. It also helped me hide the stress of waiting for what I feared might be the surprise of handcuffs.

That stress would reach its peak just ten or so minutes later, when I'd brought Laura and Glenn up to my room—#1014, on the tenth floor. Glenn had barely had the chance to stow his smartphone in my minibar fridge at my request when Laura started rearranging and adjusting the lights in the room. Then she unpacked her digital video camera. Though we'd agreed, over encrypted email, that she could film our encounter, I wasn't ready for the reality.

Nothing could have prepared me for the moment when she pointed her camera at me, sprawled out on my unmade bed in a cramped, messy room that I hadn't left for the past ten days. Though today nearly all of my interactions take place via camera, I'm still not sure which experience I find more uncomfortable: seeing myself on film or being filmed.

In a situation that was already high intensity, I stiffened. The red light of Laura's camera, like a sniper's sight, kept reminding me that at any moment the door might be smashed in and I'd be dragged off forever. And whenever I wasn't having that thought, I kept thinking about how this footage was going to look when it was played back in court. I realized there were so many things I should have done, like putting on nicer clothes and shaving. Room service plates and trash had accumulated throughout the room. There were noodle containers and half-eaten burgers, piles of dirty laundry and damp towels on the floor.

It was a surreal dynamic. I had never met any journalists before serving as their source. The first time I ever spoke aloud to anyone about the US government's system of mass surveillance, I was speaking to everyone in the world with an internet connection. In the end, though, regardless of how rumpled I looked and stilted I sounded, Laura's filming was indispensable, because it showed the world exactly what happened in that hotel room in a way that newsprint never could. The footage she shot over the course of our days together in Hong Kong can't be distorted. Its existence is a tribute not just to her professionalism as a documentarian but to her foresight.

I spent the week between June 3 and June 9 cloistered in that room with Glenn and his colleague from the *Guardian*, Ewen MacAskill, who joined us a bit later that first day. We talked and talked, going through the NSA's programs, while Laura hovered and filmed. In contrast to the frenetic days, the nights were empty and desolate. Glenn and Ewen would retreat to their own hotel, the nearby W, to write up their findings into articles. Laura would disappear to edit her footage and do her own reporting with Bart Gellman of the *Washington Post*, who never made it to Hong Kong but worked remotely with the documents he received from her.

On June 5, the *Guardian* broke Glenn's first story, the Foreign Intelligence Surveillance Act court order that authorized the NSA to collect information from the American company Verizon about every phone call it handled. On June 6, it ran another story by Glenn, pretty much simultaneously with a similar account in the *Washington Post* by Laura and Bart. I knew, and I think we all knew, that the more pieces came out the more likely it was that I'd be identified, particularly because my office had begun emailing me asking for status updates, and I wasn't answering. Glenn and Ewen and Laura were unfailingly sympathetic to my ticking time-bomb situation. But they never let their desire to serve the truth be influenced by my circumstances. And following their example, neither did I.

As the revelations ran wall to wall on every TV channel and website, it became clear that the US government had thrown the whole of its machinery into identifying the source. It was also clear that when they did, they would use the face they found—my face—to evade accountability: Instead of addressing the revelations, they'd challenge my credibility and the motives of "the leaker."

The only hope I had of fighting back was to come forward first and identify myself. I'd give the media just enough personal detail to satisfy their mounting curiosity, with a clear statement that what mattered wasn't me, but rather the subversion of American democracy. Then I'd vanish just as quickly as I'd appeared. That, at least, was the plan.

Ewen and I decided that he'd write a story about my IC career, and Laura suggested filming a video statement to appear alongside it in the *Guardian*. In it, I'd claim direct and sole responsibility as the source behind the reporting on global mass surveillance. But we just didn't have the time for her to go through everything she'd shot in search of snippets of me speaking coherently and making eye contact. What she proposed, instead, was my first recorded statement, which she started filming right there and then—the one that begins "Uh, my name is Ed Snowden. I'm, ah, twenty-nine years old."

Hello, world.

• • • • • • • •

While I've never once regretted tugging aside the curtain and revealing my identity, I do wish I had done it with better diction and a better plan in mind for what was next. In truth, I had no plan at all. I hadn't given much thought to answering the question of what to do once the game was over, mainly because a winning conclusion was always so unlikely. All I'd cared about was getting the facts out into the world. I figured that by putting the documents into the public record, I was essentially putting myself at the public's mercy. No exit strategy could be the only exit strategy.

If I'd made preexisting arrangements to fly to a specific country and seek asylum—the act of fleeing one's country for the protection of another—I would've been called a foreign agent of that country. Meanwhile, if I returned to my own country, the best I could hope for was to be arrested upon landing and charged under the Espionage Act. That would've entitled me to a show trial deprived of any meaningful defense, a sham in which all discussion of the most important facts would be forbidden. I almost certainly would've been found guilty.

The major impediment to justice was a major flaw in the law, a purposeful flaw created by the government. Someone in my position would not even be allowed to argue in court that the disclosures I made to journalists were beneficial. Even now, years after the fact, I would not be allowed to argue that the reporting based on my disclosures had caused Congress to change certain laws regarding surveillance, or convinced the courts to strike down a certain mass surveillance program as illegal, or influenced the attorney general and the president of the United States to admit that the debate over mass surveillance was a crucial one for the public to have. All these claims would be deemed not just irrelevant but inadmissible in court.

The only thing my government would have to prove is that I disclosed classified information to journalists, a fact that is not in dispute. This is why anyone who says I have to come back to the States for trial is essentially saying I have to come back to the States for sentencing. And the sentence would, now as then, surely be a cruel one. The penalty for disclosing top secret documents is up to ten years per document.

From the moment Laura's video of me was posted on the *Guardian* website on June 9, I was marked. There was a target on my back. I knew that the institutions I'd shamed would not relent until my head was bagged and my limbs were shackled. And until then—and perhaps even after then—they would harass my loved ones and disparage my character. I was familiar enough with how this process went, both from having read classified examples of it within the IC and from having studied the cases of other whistleblowers and leakers.

As sure as I was of my government's indignation, I was just as sure of the support of my family, and of Lindsay, who I was certain would understand—perhaps not forgive, but understand—the context of my recent behavior. I took comfort from recalling their love: It helped me cope with the fact that there was nothing left for me to do, no further plans in play. I could only hope that my fellow citizens, once they'd been made aware of the full scope of American mass surveillance, would mobilize and call for justice. They'd be empowered to seek that justice for themselves, and, in the process, my own destiny would be decided. This was the ultimate leap of faith: I could hardly trust anyone, so I had to trust everyone.

●　　●　　●　　●　　●　　●　　●

Within hours after my *Guardian* video ran, one of Glenn's regular readers in Hong Kong contacted him and offered to put me in touch with Robert Tibbo and Jonathan Man, two local attorneys who then volunteered to take on my case. These were the men who helped get me out of the Mira when the press finally located me and besieged the hotel. As a diversion, Glenn went out the front lobby door, where he was immediately thronged by the cameras and mics. Meanwhile, I was bundled out of one of the Mira's myriad other exits, which connected via a sky bridge to a mall.

I like Robert—to have been his client is to be his friend for life. He's an idealist and a crusader, a tireless champion of lost causes. Even more impressive than his lawyering, however, was his creativity in finding safe houses. While journalists were scouring every five-star hotel in Hong Kong, he took me to one of the poorest neighborhoods of the city and introduced me to some of his other clients, a few of the nearly twelve thousand forgotten refugees in Hong Kong. I wouldn't usually name them, but since they have bravely identified themselves to the press, I will: Vanessa Mae Bondalian Rodel from the Philippines, and Ajith Pushpakumara, Supun Thilina Kellapatha, and Nadeeka Dilrukshi Nonis, all from Sri Lanka.

These unfailingly kind and generous people came through with charitable grace. The solidarity they showed me was not political. It was human, and I will be forever in their debt. They didn't care who I was, or what dangers they might face by helping me, only that there was a person in need. They knew all too well what it meant to be forced into a mad escape from mortal threat, having survived ordeals far in excess of anything I'd dealt with and hopefully ever will. They let an exhausted stranger into their homes—and when they saw my face on TV, they didn't falter. Instead, they smiled and took the opportunity to reassure me of their hospitality.

Though their resources were limited—Supun, Nadeeka, Vanessa, and two little girls lived in a crumbling, cramped apartment smaller than my room at the Mira—they shared everything they had with me, and they shared it unstintingly, refusing my offers to reimburse them for the cost of taking me in so emphatically that I had to hide money in the room to get them to accept it. They fed me, they let me bathe, they let me sleep, and they protected me. I will never be able to explain what it meant to be given so much by those with so little, to be accepted by them without judgment as I perched in corners like a stray street cat, skimming the Wi-Fi of distant hotels with a special antenna that delighted the children.

Their welcome and friendship was a gift, for the world to even have such people is a gift, and so it pains me that, all these years later, the cases of Ajith, Supun, Nadeeka, and Nadeeka's daughter are still pending. The admiration I feel for these folks is matched only by the resentment I feel toward the bureaucrats in Hong Kong, who continue to deny them the basic dignity of asylum. What gives me hope, however, is that Vanessa and her daughter received asylum in Canada. I look forward to the day when I can visit all of my old Hong Kong friends in their new homes, wherever those may be, and we can make happier memories together in freedom.

On June 14, the US government charged me under the Espionage Act in a sealed complaint, and on June 21 they formally requested my extradition, which, under international law, means the US asked Hong Kong to return me to the States so that I could be put on trial. It was my thirtieth birthday.

Just as the US State Department sent its request, my lawyers received a reply to my appeal for assistance from the UN High Commissioner for Refugees: There was nothing that could be done for me. The Hong Kong government would not provide me international protection on its territory. In other words, Hong Kong was telling me to go home and deal with the UN from prison. I wasn't just on my own—I was unwelcome. If I was going to leave freely, I had to leave now. I wiped my four laptops completely clean and destroyed the cryptographic key, which meant that I could no longer access any of the documents even if compelled. Then I packed the few clothes I had and headed out.

TWENTY-FIVE

Moscow

For a coastal country at the northwest-ern edge of South America, half a globe away from Hong Kong, Ecuador is in the middle of everything. Most of my fellow North Americans would correctly say that it's a small country. Ecuador, at least in 2013, had a hard-earned belief in the institution of polit-ical asylum—the right of a person to live in a foreign country if they have had to leave their own country for political reasons. My Hong Kong lawyers agreed that, given the circumstances, Ecuador seemed to be the most likely country to defend my right to political asylum.

With my government having decided to charge me under the Espionage Act, I stood accused of a political crime, meaning a crime whose victim is the state itself rather than a person. Under international humanitarian law, whistleblowers should be protected against extradition—from being forcibly sent back to the country accusing them of a crime—almost everywhere. In practice, though, this is rarely the case. The most common advice my team received was for me to avoid any route that crossed the airspace of any countries with a record of cooperation with the US military.

The moment the news broke that an American had unmasked a global system of mass surveillance, Sarah Harrison, a journalist and editor for WikiLeaks, had immediately flown to Hong Kong. WikiLeaks is a nonprofit organization that publishes classified information, including news leaks, from anonymous sources on its website. Through Sarah's experience with WikiLeaks, she was poised to offer me the world's best asylum advice. It didn't hurt that she also had family connections with the legal community in Hong Kong.

Laura informed me of Sarah's presence in Hong Kong only a day or so before she communicated with me on an encrypted channel, which itself was only a day or two before I actually met her in person. Sarah managed to procure a document that would provide me safe passage to Ecuador—it was a UN-recognized one-way travel document typically issued to refugees crossing borders. It had been issued on an emergency basis, and the moment it was in hand, Sarah hired a van to take us to the airport.

That's how I met her—in motion. I'd like to say that I started off our acquaintance by offering my thanks, but instead the first thing I said was "When was the last time you slept?" Sarah looked just as ragged and disheveled as I did. She stared out the window, as if trying to recall the answer, but then just shook her head: "I don't know."

We were traveling to Quito, Ecuador, via Moscow, Russia, via Havana, Cuba, via Caracas, Venezuela, for a simple reason: It was the only safe route available. There were no direct flights to Quito from Hong Kong, and all of the other connecting flights traveled through US airspace. I was concerned about the massive layover in Russia—we'd have almost twenty hours before the Havana flight departed.

I wore my hat down over my eyes to avoid being recognized, and Sarah did the seeing for me. She took my arm and led me to the gate, where we waited until boarding. This was the last moment for her to back out, and I told her so. "You don't have to do this," I said.

"Do what?"

"Protect me like this."

Sarah stiffened. "Let's get one thing clear," she said as we boarded. "I'm not protecting you. No one can protect you. What I'm here for is to make it harder for anyone to interfere. To make sure everyone's on their best behavior."

"So you're my witness," I said.

She gave a slight wry smile. "Someone has to be the last person to ever see you alive. It might as well be me."

Though the three points where I'd thought we were most likely to get stopped were now behind us (check-in, passport control, and the gate), I didn't feel safe on the plane. I didn't want to get complacent. I took the window seat, and Sarah sat next to me to screen me from the other passengers across the row. After what felt like an eternity, the cabin doors were shut, the sky bridge pulled away, and finally, we were moving.

But just before the plane rolled from the tarmac onto the runway, it halted sharply. I was nervous. Pressing the brim of my hat up against the glass, I strained to catch the sound of sirens or the flashing of blue lights. It felt like I was playing the waiting game all over again—it was a wait that wouldn't end. Until, suddenly, the plane rolled into motion again and took a turn, and I realized that we were just far back in the line for takeoff.

My spirits rose with the wheels, but it was hard to believe I was out of the fire. Once we were airborne, I loosened my grip from my thighs and felt an urge to take my lucky Rubik's Cube out of my bag. But I knew I

couldn't, because nothing would make me more conspic-
uous now that tales of my Rubik's Cube had spread far
and wide. Instead, I sat back, pulled my hat down again,
and kept my half-open eyes on the map on the seat-back
screen just in front of me, tracking the pixelated route
across China, Mongolia, and Russia.

There was no predicting what the Russian government would do once we landed, beyond hauling us into
an inspection so they could search through my blank
laptops and empty bag. What I hoped might spare us
any more invasive treatment was that the world was
watching, and my lawyers were aware of our itinerary.

• • • • • • • •

We landed at Sheremetyevo International Airport on
June 23 for what we assumed would be a twenty-hour
layover. It has now dragged on for over seven years.
Exile is an endless layover.

In the IC, and in the CIA in particular, you get a lot of
training on how not to get into trouble at customs. You
have to think about how you dress, how you act. You have
to think about the things in your bag and the things in
your pockets and the tales they tell about you. Your goal
is to be the most boring person in line, with the most
perfectly forgettable face. But none of that really matters
when the name on your passport is all over the news.

I handed my little blue book to the guy in the passport-control booth, who scanned it and rifled through its pages. Sarah stood stalwart behind me. I'd made sure to take note of the time it took for the people ahead of us in line to clear the booth, and our turn was taking too long. Then the guy picked up his phone, grumbled some words in Russian, and almost immediately—far too quickly—two security officers in suits approached. They must have been waiting. The officer in front took my little blue book from the guy in the booth and leaned in close to me. "There is problem with passport," he said. "Please, come with."

Sarah immediately stepped to my side and unleashed a fast flurry of English: "I'm his legal adviser. Wherever he goes, I go. I'm coming with you. According to the—"

But before she could cite the relevant information, the officer held up his hand and glanced at the line. He said, "Okay, sure, okay. You come."

I don't know whether the officer had even under-stood what she said. He just clearly didn't want to make a scene.

The two security officers marched us briskly toward what I assumed was going to be a special room for sec-ondary inspection but instead turned out to be one of Sheremetyevo's plush business lounges—like a business-class or first-class area, with just a few passengers basking obliviously in their luxury seats. Sarah and I were directed past them and down a hall into a conference room of sorts, filled with men in gray sitting around a table. There were a half dozen of them or so, with military haircuts. One guy sat separately, holding a pen. He was a note taker, a kind of secretary, I guessed. He had a folder in front of him containing a pad of paper. On the cover of the folder was a monochrome insignia that I didn't need Russian in order to understand: It was a sword and shield, the symbol of Russia's foremost intelligence service, the Federal Security Service (FSB). Like the FBI in the United States, the FSB exists not only to spy and investigate but also to make arrests.

At the center of the table sat an older man in a finer suit than the others, the white of his hair shining like a halo of authority. He gestured for Sarah and me to sit opposite him with an authoritative sweep of the hand and a smile that marked him as a seasoned case officer. Intelligence services the world over are full of such figures—dedicated actors who will try on different emotions until they get the response they want.

He cleared his throat and gave me, in decent English, what the CIA calls a cold pitch, which is basically an offer by a foreign intelligence service that can be summarized as "come and work for us." In return for cooperation, the foreigners dangle favors, which can be anything from stacks of cash to a get-out-of-jail-free card for pretty much anything from fraud to murder. The catch, of course, is that the foreigners always expect something of equal or better value in exchange.

I knew I had to cut him off. If you don't cut off a foreign intelligence officer right away, it might not matter whether you ultimately reject their offer, because they can destroy your reputation simply by leaking a recording of you considering it. So as the man apologized for inconveniencing us, I imagined the hidden devices recording us and tried to choose my words carefully.

"Listen, I understand who you are, and what this is," I said. "Please let me be clear that I have no intention to cooperate with you. I'm not going to cooperate with any intelligence service. I mean no disrespect, but this isn't going to be that kind of meeting. If you want to search my bag, it's right here." And I pointed to it under my chair. "But I promise you, there's nothing in it that can help you."

As I was speaking, the man's face changed. He started to act wounded. "No, we would never do that," he said. "Please believe me, we only want to help you."

Sarah cleared her throat and jumped in. "That's quite kind of you, but I hope you can understand that all we'd like is to make our connecting flight."

For the briefest instant, the man's feigned sorrow became irritation. "You are his lawyer?"

"I'm his legal adviser," Sarah answered.

The man asked me, "So you are not coming to Russia to be in Russia?"

"No."

"And so may I ask where you are trying to go? What is your final destination?"

I said, "Quito, Ecuador, via Caracas, via Havana," even though I knew that he already knew the answer. He certainly had a copy of our itinerary, since Sarah and I had traveled from Hong Kong on Aeroflot, the Russian flagship airline.

Up until this point, he and I had been reading from the same intelligence script, but now the conversation swerved. "You haven't heard?" he said. He stood and looked at me like he was delivering the news of a death in the family. "I am afraid to inform you that your passport is invalid."

I was so surprised, I just stammered. "I'm sorry, but I—I don't believe that."

The man leaned over the table and said, "No, it is true. Believe me. It is the decision of your minister, John Kerry. Your passport has been canceled by your government, and the air services have been instructed not to allow you to travel."

I was sure it was a trick, but I wasn't quite sure to what purpose. "Give us a minute," I said, but even before I could ask, Sarah had snatched her laptop out of her bag and was getting onto the airport Wi-Fi.

"Of course, you will check," the man said, and he turned to his colleagues and chatted amiably to them in Russian, as if he had all the time in the world.

It was reported on every site Sarah looked at. After the news had broken that I'd left Hong Kong, the US State Department announced that it had canceled my passport. It had revoked my travel document while I was still in midair.

"It's true," said Sarah, with a shake of her head. I was incredulous: My own government had trapped me in Russia.

"So what will you do?" the man asked, and he walked around to our side of the table.

Before I could take the Ecuadorean safe-conduct pass out of my pocket, Sarah said, "I'm so sorry, but I'm going to have to advise Mr. Snowden not to answer any more questions."

The man pointed at me, and said, "You will come."

He gestured for me to follow him to the far end of the conference room, where there was a window. I went and stood next to him and looked. About three or four floors below was street level and the largest media scrum I've ever seen, scads of reporters wielding cameras and mics.

I went back to my chair but didn't sit down again.

The man turned from the window to face me and

said, "Life for a person in your situation can be very difficult without friends who can help." He let the words linger.

Here it comes, I thought—the direct solicitation.

He said, "If there is some information, perhaps, some small thing you could share with us?"

"We'll be okay on our own," I said. Sarah stood up next to me.

The man sighed. He turned to mumble in Russian, and his comrades rose and filed out. "I hope you will not regret your decision," he said to me. Then he gave a slight bow and made his own exit, just as a pair of officials from the airport administration entered.

I demanded to be allowed to go to the gate for the flight to Havana, but they ignored me. I finally reached into my pocket and brandished the Ecuadorean safe-conduct pass, but they ignored that, too.

All told, we were trapped in the airport for a biblical forty days and forty nights. Over the course of those days, I applied to a total of twenty-seven countries for political asylum. Not a single one of them was willing to stand up to American pressure, with some countries refusing outright and others declaring that they were unable to even consider my request until I arrived in their territory—a feat that was impossible. Ultimately, the only head of state that proved sympathetic to my cause was

Burger King, who never denied me a Whopper (hold the tomato and onion).

Soon, my presence in the airport became a global spectacle. Eventually the Russians found it a nuisance. The Russian government must have decided that it would be better off without me and the media swarm clogging up the country's major airport. On August 1, it granted me temporary asylum. Sarah and I were allowed to leave Sheremetyevo, but eventually only one of us would be heading home. Our time together served to bind us as friends for life. I will always be grateful for the weeks she spent by my side, for her integrity and her fortitude.

TWENTY-SIX

From the Diaries of Lindsay Mills

As far away from home as I was, my thoughts were consumed with Lindsay. I've been wary of telling her story—the story of what happened to her once I was gone: the FBI interrogations, the surveillance, the press attention, the online harassment, the confusion and pain, the anger and sadness. Finally, I realized that only Lindsay herself should be the person to recount that period. No one else has the experience, but more than that, no one else has the right. Luckily, Lindsay has long kept a diary, using it to record her life and draft her art. She has graciously agreed to let me include a few pages, which can be accessed via the QR code or URL below. In the entries, all names have been changed (except those of family), some typos fixed, and a few redactions made. Otherwise, this is how it was, from the moment that I left Hawaii.

read.macmillan.com/mcpg/permanentrecordbonus/

TWENTY-SEVEN

Love and Exile

I F AT ANY POINT DURING YOUR JOURNEY THROUGH this book you paused for a moment over a term you wanted to clarify or investigate further and typed it into a search engine—and if that term happened to be in some way suspicious—then congrats: You're in the system, a victim of your own curiosity.

But even if you didn't search for anything online, it wouldn't take much for an interested government to find out that you've been reading this book. At the very least, it wouldn't take much to find out that you have it, whether you bought a hard copy online or purchased it at a brick-and-mortar store with a credit card.

All you wanted to do was read. But that was more

than enough. By creating a world-spanning system that tracked identifiers like your email, your phone, and the IP address of your computer across every available channel of electronic communications, the American Intelligence Community gave itself the power to record and store forever the data of your life.

And that was only the beginning. Because once America's spy agencies had proven to themselves that it was possible to passively collect all of your communications, they started actively tampering with them, too. By poisoning the messages that were headed your way with snippets of attack code, they developed the ability to gain possession of more than just your words. Now they were capable of winning total control of your whole device, including its camera and microphone. Which means that if you're reading this now—this sentence—on any sort of modern machine, like a smartphone or tablet, they can follow along and *read you*. They can tell how quickly or slowly you turn the pages and whether you read the chapters consecutively or skip around. But what they really want is the data that lets them positively identify you.

This is the result of two decades of unchecked innovation. No matter the place, no matter the time, and no matter what you do, your life has now become an open book.

. . . .

If mass surveillance was, by definition, a constant presence in daily life, then I wanted the dangers it posed, and the damage it had already done, to be a constant presence, too. Through my disclosures to the press, I wanted to make this system known, its existence a fact that my country, and the world, could not ignore. In the years since 2013, awareness has grown. But in this social media age, we have always to remind ourselves: Awareness alone is not enough.

Because of the revelations of 2013, both houses of Congress launched multiple investigations into NSA abuses. Those investigations concluded that the agency had repeatedly lied regarding the nature and efficacy of its mass surveillance programs, even to the most highly cleared Intelligence Committee legislators.

In 2015, a federal court of appeals ruled in the lawsuit *ACLU v. Clapper*, which challenged the legality of the NSA's phone records collection program. The court ruled that the NSA's program had violated the Patriot Act and, moreover, was most probably unconstitutional.

ACLU v. Clapper was a notable victory, to be sure. A crucial precedent was set. The court declared that the American public had standing: American citizens had the right to stand in a court of law and challenge the

government's officially secret system of mass surveillance. But it becomes ever clearer to me that an international opposition movement, fully implemented across
both governments and private sector is what's needed.

Apple has adopted strong default encryption for its
iPhones and iPads, and Google followed suit for its
Android products and Chromebooks. Perhaps the most
important private-sector change occurred when businesses throughout the world set about switching their
website platforms, replacing HTTP (Hypertext Transfer
Protocol) with the encrypted HTTPS (the S signifies
security), which helps prevent third-party interception of
Web traffic. 2016 was the first year since the invention
of the internet that more Web traffic was encrypted than
unencrypted.

The internet is certainly more secure now than it
was in 2013, especially given the sudden global recognition of the need for encrypted tools and apps. I've
been involved with the design and creation of a few of
these myself, through my work heading the Freedom of
the Press Foundation, a nonprofit organization dedicated
to protecting and empowering public-interest journalism in the new millennium. A major goal of the organization is to preserve and strengthen First and Fourth
Amendment rights through the development of encryption technologies.

In my current situation, I'm constantly reminded of

the fact that the law is country specific, whereas technology is not. Every nation has its own legal code but the same computer code. Technology crosses borders and carries almost every passport. As the years go by, it has become increasingly apparent to me that changing surveillance practices and laws in the US won't necessarily help a journalist in Russia, but an encrypted smartphone might.

· · · · · · ·

Internationally, the disclosures helped to revive debates about surveillance. For the first time since the end of World War II, liberal democratic governments throughout the world were discussing privacy as the natural, inborn right of every man, woman, and child. The European Union became the first transnational body to establish a new directive that seeks to standardize whistleblower protections across its member states, along with a standardized legal framework for privacy protection. In 2016, the European Parliament passed the General Data Protection Regulation (GDPR).

The GDPR treats the citizens of the European Union, whom it calls "natural persons," as also being "data subjects"—that is, people who generate personally identifiable data. In the US, data is usually regarded as the property of whoever collects it.

Today, no matter who you are, or where you are

physically, you are also elsewhere. Our data wanders far and wide. Our data wanders endlessly.

We start generating this data before we are born, when technologies detect us in utero, and our data will continue to proliferate even after we die. Of course, our consciously created memories, the records that we choose to keep, comprise just a sliver of the information that has been wrung out of our lives—most of it unconsciously, or without our consent—by business and government surveillance. We are the first people in the history of the planet for whom this is true, the first people to be burdened with data immortality. This is why we have a special duty. We must ensure that these records of our pasts can't be turned against us, or turned against our future children.

Today, a generation that wasn't yet born when 9/11 took place, those whose entire lives have been spent under the omnipresent specter of this surveillance, is championing privacy. Their political creativity and technological ingenuity give me hope. You, the readers of this book, give me hope.

If we don't reclaim our data now, future generations might not be able to do so. Then they, and their children, will be trapped, too.

Who among us can predict the future? Who would dare to? The answer to the first question is no one, really, and the answer to the second is everyone, especially every government and business on the planet. This is what that data of ours is used for. Algorithms analyze it for patterns of established behavior. A website that tells you that because you liked this book you might also like books by author A or author B isn't offering an educated guess as much as a tool of subtle pressure and influence.

We can't allow ourselves to be used in this way. We can't permit our data to be used against us. We can't let the godlike surveillance we're under be used to "predict" our criminal activity. And as for our genetic information, our most intimate data: If we allow it to be used to identify us, then it will be used to victimize us, even to modify us.

Of course, all of the above has already happened.

• • • • • • •

Exile: When people ask me what my life is like now, I tend to answer that it's a lot like theirs in that I spend a lot of time in front of the computer—reading, writing, interacting. From what the press likes to describe as an "undisclosed location"—which is really just whatever two-bedroom apartment in Moscow I happen to be renting—I beam myself onto stages around the world, speaking about the protection of civil liberties in the digital age to audiences of students, scholars, lawmakers, and technologists.

Some days I take virtual meetings. Other days I just pick up some Burger King. One fixture of my existence is my daily check-in with my American lawyer, confidant, and all-around consigliere Ben Wizner at the ACLU, who has been my guide to the world as it is and puts up with my musings about the world as it should be.

That's my life. It got significantly brighter during the freezing winter of 2014, when Lindsay came to visit—the first time I'd seen her since Hawaii.

From the moment she arrived, my world was hers. Previously, I'd been content to hang around indoors—indeed, that was my preference—but Lindsay was insistent: She'd never been to Russia, and now we were going to be tourists together.

My Russian lawyer, Anatoly Kucherena, who helped me get asylum in the country, arranged two box seats at the Bolshoi Theatre. Lindsay and I got dressed and went, though I have to admit I was wary. There were so many people, all packed so tightly into a hall. Lindsay could sense my growing unease. As the lights dimmed and the curtain rose, she leaned over, nudged me in the ribs, and whispered, "None of these people are here for you. They're here for this."

Lindsay and I also spent time at some of Moscow's

museums. At the Tretyakov Gallery, a young tourist, a teenage girl, suddenly stepped between us. This wasn't the first time I'd been recognized in public, but given Lindsay's presence, it certainly threatened to be the most headline worthy. In German-accented English, the girl asked whether she could take a selfie with us. I'm not sure what explains my reaction, but without hesitation, for once, I agreed. Lindsay smiled as the girl posed between us and took a photo. Then, after a few sweet words of support, she departed.

I dragged Lindsay out of the museum a moment later. I was afraid that if the girl posted the photo to social media, we could be just minutes away from unwanted attention. I feel foolish now for thinking that. I kept nervously checking online, but the photo didn't appear. Not that day, and not the day after. As far as I can tell, it was never shared—just kept as a private memory of a personal moment.

•   •   •   •   •   •   •

Whenever I go outside, I try to change my appearance a bit. Maybe I get rid of my beard; maybe I wear different glasses. I never liked the cold until I realized that a hat and scarf provide the world's most convenient and inconspicuous anonymity. I change the rhythm and pace of my walk and look away from traffic when crossing the street, which is why I've never been caught on any of the car dash cams that are ubiquitous here. Passing buildings equipped with CCTV, I keep my head down, so that no one will see me as I'm usually seen online—head on. I used to worry about the bus and metro, but nowadays everybody's too busy staring at their phones to give me a second glance. If I take a cab, I'll have it pick me up at a bus or metro stop a few blocks away from where I live and drop me off at an address a few blocks away from where I'm going.

Today, I'm taking the long way around this vast, strange city, trying to find some roses. Red roses, white roses, even blue violets. Any flowers I can find. I don't know the Russian names of any of them. I just grunt and point.

Lindsay's Russian is better than mine. She also laughs more easily and is more patient and generous and kind.

Tonight, we're celebrating our wedding anniversary. Yes, reader, she married me.

AFTERWORD

IF YOU'VE GOTTEN TO THIS CHAPTER, THEN YOU'VE done better than I did back in my school days. But even after reading every single chapter, you might still have some basic questions, such as: What can I do to protect my digital privacy as well as my family's and friends', and to protect our basic freedoms? It's fine to make sweeping arguments about the need for technological and legal reforms, but what about some more practical information?

But there's a problem with practical information: It tends to change, and to change rather quickly. If your goal is to keep yourself safe while using the internet, then you're going to have to move at the pace of the internet. This is the main burden of being a young person, in any age: The young are always living at the cutting edge.

So let me try to find a way to talk about the practical in terms other than best practices. Let me try to talk about change, because the struggle that begins with you changing your own habits must ultimately end with changes to technology, and changes to law—with change being brought to the world.

Every time you go online, you need to know the current rules of the game if you want to have any chance of controlling what happens next. You should be aware of the strengths and weaknesses of the tools you rely on to connect and protect you, along with the many ways the sites and systems on the other end intend to track and exploit you. Two organizations that I trust, the Electronic Frontier Foundation (eff.org) and the Freedom of the Press Foundation (freedom.press), publish useful guides that can get you up to speed on surveillance self-defense, from scrubbing the identifying tags invisibly hidden in your photos by your phone to encrypting your data with even better techniques than the ones I used to stand up against the NSA.

Once a solid foundation is acquired, you might want to get involved with the Open Source movement. A great way of doing that is through the Free Software Foundation (fsf.org).

To get involved in the ongoing discussions of technology's intersections with civil liberties, you can't do better than seeking out the ACLU (aclu.org); for technology's intersection with climate science, I'd recommend 350.org.

When I started thinking about putting together a version of my book for younger readers, I realized that I wanted to write a final chapter directly addressing my own protocols—the steps I take to keep secure online—a subject I'm continually asked about. When I sat down to write this book, I didn't just open up a Microsoft Word document and type in it, and then attach the document to an email to my publisher sent from an account like edwardjsnowden@gmail.com or Sys-Admin@apple.com. Instead, I wrote it in an Open Source word-processing program, LibreOffice Writer, running on a "virtual machine" that never connects to the internet. I then encrypted the finished document, transferred the encrypted copy to write-once media, which I then moved onto a different computer that goes online only through the anonymity-friendly Tor network. From there, I uploaded the encrypted file to a file-sharing site that doesn't require a log-in, and using another virtual machine pretending to be a phone, I sent the password to the encrypted file to my publisher using the Signal messenger.

If that sounds like babble to you, remember that there was a time when none of it meant anything to me, either. Besides, sometimes you aren't trying to beat the NSA, you're just trying to keep your kid brother or sister out of your browsing history or a jealous ex from stalking you. You yourself may not have to go through every step of this process in order to just send an email, but maybe a single technique—whether you're protecting your identity, your location, your contacts, or just the content of what you say and share online—will one day be of help.

In general, I think it's important to remember that no matter how quickly the internet changes, you yourself change, too. Some of the best advice I can give is to start thinking about the future as you already think about the past: You know you've changed so much in the past decade, so imagine how much you will continue to change as you get older. So much of good online habits come from merely recalling this fact, and the importance of giving yourself the opportunity to reinvent who you are. This involves a significant amount of self-forgiveness, for example, forgiving yourself for past views that you expressed online but may no longer hold, but it also involves extending that forgiveness to others, who are surely going through the same process of continuous growth.

Ultimately, our privacy is collective: Yours depends on your classmates' and friends', and theirs depends on yours. Remember that anything you share can be reshared and eventually reach the eyes and ears of those for whom it was never originally intended. We should never make assumptions about people, least of all about what they consider public or private or secret. A good steward is a perennial good student: someone who's never too afraid to ask, *Can I share this and with whom? When and where, if and how?*

ACKNOWLEDGMENTS

In May 2013, as I sat in that hotel room in Hong Kong wondering whether any journalists would show up to meet me, I'd never felt more alone. Seven years later, I find myself in quite the opposite situation, having been welcomed into an extraordinary and ever-expanding global tribe of journalists, lawyers, technologists, and human rights advocates to whom I owe an incalculable debt. At the conclusion of a book, it's traditional for an author to thank the people who helped make the book possible, and I certainly intend to do that here, but given the circumstances, I'd be remiss if I didn't also thank the people who have helped make my life possible—by advocating for my freedom and, especially, by working ceaselessly and selflessly to protect our open societies as well as the technologies that have brought us, and that bring everyone, together.

Over the last nine months, Joshua Cohen has taken me to writing school, helping to transform my rambling reminiscences and capsule manifestos into a book that I hope he can be proud of.

Chris Parris-Lamb proved himself a shrewd and patient agent, while Sam Nicholson provided astute and clarifying edits and support, as did the entire team at Macmillan, from Gillian Blake to Sara Bershtel, Riva Hocherman, Grigory Tovbis, and Brian Geffen. Thank you, Catherine Frank, for your help on the young readers adaptation.

The success of this team is a testament to its members' talents, and to the talents of the man who assembled it— Ben Wizner, my lawyer, and, I am honored to say, my friend.

In the same vein, I'd like to thank my international team of lawyers who have worked tirelessly to keep me free. I would also like to thank Anthony Romero, the ACLU's director, who embraced my cause at a time of considerable political risk for the organization, along with the other ACLU staff who have helped me throughout the years, including Bennett Stein, Nicola Morrow, Noa Yachot, and Daniel Kahn Gillmor.

Additionally, I'd like to acknowledge the work of Bob Walker, Jan Tavitian, and their team at the American Program Bureau, who have allowed me to make a living by spreading my message to new audiences around the world.

Trevor Timm and my fellow board members at the Freedom of the Press Foundation have provided the space and resources for me to return to my true passion, engineering for social good. I am especially grateful to our CTO Micah Lee, former FPF operations manager Emmanuel Morales, and current FPF board member Daniel Ellsberg, who has given the world the model of his rectitude, and given me the warmth and candor of his friendship.

This book was written using free and open-source software. I would like thank the Qubes Project, the Tor Project, and the Free Software Foundation.

My earliest intimations of what it was like to write against deadline came from the masters, Glenn Greenwald, Laura Poitras, Ewen MacAskill, and Bart Gellman, whose professionalism is informed by a passionate integrity. Having been edited now myself, I have gained a new appreciation of their editors, who refused to be intimidated and took the risks that gave meaning to their principles.

My deepest gratitude is reserved for Sarah Harrison.

And my heart belongs to my family, extended and immediate—to my father, Lon; to my mother, Wendy; and to my brilliant sister, Jessica.

The only way I can end this book is the way I began it: with a dedication to Lindsay, whose love makes life out of exile.

ABOUT THE AUTHOR

EDWARD SNOWDEN WAS BORN IN ELIZABETH CITY, North Carolina, and grew up in the shadow of Fort Meade. A systems engineer by training, he served as an officer of the Central Intelligence Agency and worked as a contractor for the National Security Agency. He has received numerous awards for his public service, including the Right Livelihood Award, the German Whistleblower Prize, the Ridenhour Prize for Truth-Telling, and the Carl von Ossietzky Medal from the International League of Human Rights. Currently, he serves as president of the board of directors of the Freedom of the Press Foundation.